Mastering
Home
Automation

A DIY Guide to Smart Home Projects

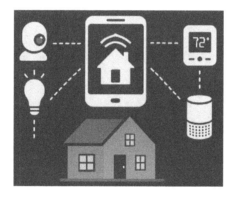

AUTHOR

GERALD CAROLINO

"Mastering Home Automation: A DIY Guide to Smart Home Projects,"

ISBN: 9798280122185
Imprint: Independently published

Disclaimer

This publication, *Mastering Home Automation: A DIY Guide to Smart Home Projects*, is intended for informational and educational purposes only. The author and publisher have made every effort to ensure the accuracy of the information contained herein. However, they assume no responsibility for errors, omissions, or outcomes resulting from the use of this information.

DIY smart home projects may involve risks, including but not limited to electrical work, cybersecurity considerations, and structural modifications. It is the responsibility of the reader to consult with appropriate professionals, adhere to local building codes and regulations, and observe all necessary safety precautions.

The author and publisher disclaim any liability for any loss, damage, or injury caused directly or indirectly by the information presented in this guide.

This guide is independently authored and not sponsored or endorsed by any brands or manufacturers mentioned.

By using this guide, you accept full responsibility for any and all outcomes resulting from your actions.

Dedication

To the innovators, tinkerers, and problem-solvers who turn houses into smart homes—may your creativity and curiosity continue to push the boundaries of technology.

To my family and friends, whose support and patience made this journey possible.

And to all DIY enthusiasts, may this guide inspire you to build, learn, and automate with confidence.

Table of Contents

Mastering i

A DIY Guide to Smart Home Projects i

Disclaimer iii

Dedication...v

Table of Contents vii

Preface 9

Introduction: The Smart Home Revolution 11

Chapter 1: Getting Started with Home Automation...25

Chapter 2: Wiring and Setting Up Smart Lights 55

Chapter 3: DIY Smart Thermostat Installation.........88

Chapter 4: Building Your Own Smart Security System
....122

Chapter 5: Voice Control Setup and Automation 150

Chapter 6: Home Automation for Energy Management

....186

Chapter 7: Building a Smart Garden....................226

Chapter 8: Troubleshooting and Maintenance 260

Conclusion and Next Steps..............................281

Appendix Smart Sensing Devices and Their Functions
....300

Appendix Smart Wireless Security Systems 302

Appendix Smart Bulb and Plug Wiring Diagram 305

Appendix Zigbee Layout 306

Appendix Z-Wave Layout...............................308

Report: Mastering Home Automation: A DIY Guide to
Smart Home Projects 310

Epilogue 315

Acknowledgments..317

Author 319

Call to Action 321

Preface

The concept of a smart home was once a futuristic dream, but today, it is more accessible than ever. With advancements in technology, anyone can automate their home, improving convenience, security, and efficiency. *Mastering Home Automation: A DIY Guide to Smart Home Projects* is designed to help beginners and tech enthusiasts navigate the world of smart home solutions.

This book is a step-by-step guide to building and customizing smart home systems without requiring professional expertise. From controlling lights with voice commands to automating security systems, each project is crafted to be practical, affordable, and adaptable to different home setups. Whether you are looking to enhance comfort, increase energy efficiency, or simply explore the potential of smart technology, this guide will empower you to take control of your home automation journey.

Through clear instructions, useful tips, and troubleshooting advice, this book aims to make home automation an enjoyable and rewarding experience. No matter your skill level, there is something here for you—whether you are just getting started or looking to expand your existing setup.

Welcome to the future of home living—designed by you.

Introduction: The Smart Home Revolution

In the not-so-distant past, the idea of a home that could anticipate your needs, respond to your voice commands, or manage itself efficiently existed only in science fiction. Today, that vision has become an accessible reality. Welcome to the world of home automation—where technology seamlessly integrates with your living space to create environments that are more comfortable, efficient, secure, and responsive than ever before.

The concept of a "smart home" has evolved from a luxury for the tech-elite to an achievable goal for the average homeowner. What began with simple programmable thermostats has blossomed into an ecosystem of interconnected devices that can transform nearly every aspect of home life. Lights that adjust based on your preferences and presence, doors that lock and unlock automatically, appliances that optimize their energy usage, and security systems that provide peace of mind from anywhere in the world— these are no longer futuristic fantasies but practical realities.

This book, "Mastering Home Automation: A DIY Guide to Smart Home Projects," is designed to be your companion on the journey from a conventional house to a personalized smart home. But unlike many resources that focus on expensive, pre-packaged solutions, our approach centers on affordable, customizable projects that you can implement yourself, even if you have limited technical experience.

The Evolution of Home Automation

The story of home automation begins decades ago, with the first rudimentary systems appearing in the 1970s. The X10 protocol, developed in 1975, represented one of the earliest standards for home automation, allowing simple control of electrical devices through existing power lines. Though primitive by today's standards, X10 laid the groundwork for what would become a technological revolution.

The 1990s saw the emergence of more sophisticated systems, though these remained largely out of reach for most consumers due to high costs and complex installation requirements. Often, these systems required professional installation, custom programming, and significant financial investment— making them accessible only to luxury homeowners and tech enthusiasts.

The true democratization of home automation began in the early 2000s, accelerating dramatically with the smartphone revolution. Suddenly, powerful computing capability was in everyone's pocket, creating the perfect control interface for smart home technology. Simultaneously, advances in wireless technologies like

Wi-Fi, Bluetooth, Zigbee, and Z-Wave eliminated the need for extensive rewiring, while cloud computing provided the backbone for more intelligent, responsive systems.

The introduction of voice assistants—Amazon's Alexa in 2014, followed by Google Assistant and Apple's expanded HomeKit ecosystem—marked another watershed moment. These platforms made interaction with smart homes more natural and intuitive, further reducing the technical barriers to entry.

Today, we stand at an exciting juncture where home automation technology has become more affordable, user-friendly, and powerful than ever before. The average consumer now has access to capabilities that would have seemed miraculous just a decade ago, and the DIY smart home movement has gained tremendous momentum.

The Benefits of Smart Home Technology

Why are so many homeowners embracing smart technology? The benefits extend far beyond the novelty factor or technological curiosity:

Enhanced Convenience and Comfort

Smart homes fundamentally transform everyday interactions with your living space. Imagine arriving home to find your house already adjusted to your preferences—lights dimmed to your favorite setting, temperature comfortable, perhaps even your preferred music playing softly in the background. Picture getting into bed and saying a single command that ensures all doors are locked, security systems are armed, and unnecessary lights and appliances are powered down.

These conveniences might seem small individually, but collectively they create a living experience that feels effortlessly personalized. From automated morning routines that synchronize with your alarm to entertainment systems that remember every family member's preferences, smart technology reduces friction in daily life.

Significant Energy Efficiency

In an era of growing environmental awareness and rising energy costs, the efficiency benefits of smart home technology are increasingly compelling. Smart thermostats learn your schedule and preferences, optimizing heating and cooling cycles to reduce energy consumption without sacrificing comfort. Intelligent lighting systems ensure lights aren't left on in unoccupied rooms, while smart power strips eliminate the vampire power draw from devices in standby mode.

Studies have shown that thoughtfully implemented smart home systems can reduce energy consumption by 10-30%, translating to meaningful cost savings and reduced environmental impact. A smart home gives you unprecedented visibility into your energy usage patterns, empowering you to make informed decisions about consumption.

Enhanced Security and Peace of Mind

Perhaps no aspect of home automation offers more tangible value than enhanced security. Smart security systems combine multiple elements—cameras, motion sensors, door/window sensors, smart locks, and more—to create comprehensive protection that traditional systems can't match.

The ability to remotely monitor your home, receive real-time alerts about unusual activity, and even communicate with visitors at your door from anywhere in the world transforms home security from a passive system to an active one. Whether you're checking in on pets during the workday, verifying that your teenager arrived home safely from school, or ensuring your vacation home remains secure during the off-season, smart security provides constant connection and peace of mind.

Aging in Place and Accessibility

Smart home technology can be life-changing for elderly individuals and those with disabilities. Voice control eliminates the need to physically interact with switches and controls. Automated lighting reduces fall risks. Smart medication dispensers provide timely reminders. Video doorbells allow screening visitors without rushing to the door.

These capabilities support independence and dignity, often allowing people to remain in their homes longer than would otherwise be possible. As our population ages, this aspect of smart home technology will only grow in importance.

Home Value and Appeal

As smart homes become more mainstream, their technology increasingly influences property values. A 2021 survey by the National Association of Realtors found that 69% of buyers would pay more for homes with smart technology installed. Beyond immediate resale value, smart homes typically spend less time on the market, giving sellers a competitive advantage.

For rental property owners, smart features can justify higher rental rates and attract quality tenants, particularly in competitive markets where differentiation matters.

The Challenges of Home Automation

Despite these compelling benefits, home automation adoption still faces several challenges:

Perceived Technical Complexity

Many potential smart home enthusiasts remain on the sidelines, intimidated by what they perceive as complex technology requiring specialized knowledge. The prospect of troubleshooting networking issues, managing firmware updates, or integrating devices from different manufacturers can seem daunting.

Cost Barriers

While prices have decreased dramatically, the upfront investment in smart home technology can still be substantial if approached without strategy. Premium, all-in-one systems from major brands often come with premium price tags that put them out of reach for budget-conscious consumers.

Privacy and Security Concerns

Smart homes generate data—lots of data. This raises legitimate questions about who has access to information about your habits, movements, and preferences. Security vulnerabilities in poorly designed devices have led to high-profile incidents where smart home systems were compromised, fueling concerns about digital safety.

Compatibility and Integration

The smart home ecosystem remains fragmented, with competing standards and platforms that don't always play well together. Consumers may find themselves locked into particular ecosystems or facing compatibility challenges when attempting to integrate devices from different manufacturers.

How This Book Will Help

This is where "Mastering Home Automation" distinguishes itself from other resources. We've designed this guide specifically to address these common challenges, making the smart home journey accessible to everyone, regardless of technical background or budget constraints.

Demystifying the Technology

Throughout this book, we'll break down complex concepts into understandable components, explaining not just what to do but why you're doing it. You'll learn the fundamental principles that underpin all smart home technology, gaining confidence to troubleshoot issues and expand your system over time.

We avoid unnecessary jargon, and when technical terms are unavoidable, we explain them clearly. The goal is to empower you with knowledge, not overwhelm you with terminology.

Budget-Friendly Approaches

Every project in this book includes options for different budget levels, from ultra-economical solutions to more feature-rich alternatives for those with greater financial flexibility. You'll learn:

- How to identify where smart technology provides the most value for your specific needs
- Strategic approaches to phased implementation that spread costs over time
- Ways to repurpose existing technology you may already own
- How to evaluate when premium products justify their cost and when budget alternatives offer better value

Prioritizing Privacy and Security

We take security seriously, providing detailed guidance on:

- Properly securing your home network, the foundation of any smart home
- Evaluating the privacy policies of different manufacturers and services
- Implementing best practices for protecting your data
- Understanding the privacy implications of different technologies
- Creating systems that maximize utility while minimizing unnecessary data collection

Achieving Integration and Harmony

Perhaps the most valuable aspect of our approach is the focus on creating integrated systems where devices work together harmoniously, rather than as isolated gadgets. You'll learn:

- How to select platforms and devices with compatibility in mind
- Techniques for bridging different ecosystems when necessary
- Methods for creating automated routines that leverage multiple devices
- Approaches to centralizing control for a cohesive user experience

The DIY Advantage

Why take the DIY approach rather than hiring professionals or purchasing pre-packaged systems? The advantages are significant:

Cost Savings

By implementing smart home technology yourself, you'll save thousands of dollars in professional installation fees. More importantly, you'll develop the skills to expand and maintain your system independently, avoiding ongoing service charges.

Customization

Pre-packaged smart home solutions are designed for the average user, but your home and needs aren't average—they're unique. The DIY approach allows you to tailor every aspect of your smart home to your specific preferences, priorities, and living patterns.

Knowledge and Control

When you understand how your smart home works from the ground up, you gain true ownership of the technology. This knowledge translates to better troubleshooting, more effective customization, and the ability to make informed decisions about future additions and changes.

Gradual Implementation

The DIY approach allows for thoughtful, incremental expansion. You can start with the areas of greatest impact, learn from each implementation, and grow your system organically rather than committing to a comprehensive solution upfront.

How to Use This Book

This book is structured to support both systematic reading and as-needed reference:

- **Foundation chapters** provide essential knowledge about networking, protocols, security, and planning that apply across all projects
- **Project-based chapters** offer step-by-step guidance for specific implementations, from basic lighting automation to comprehensive security systems
- **Advanced sections** explore more complex integrations for those ready to take their smart home to the next level
- **Troubleshooting guides** help you diagnose and resolve common issues that may arise

We recommend beginning with the foundation chapters to build a solid understanding of key principles before diving into specific projects. However, if you're eager to see quick results, many early projects can be implemented successfully even while you're building your knowledge base.

Each project includes:

- A clear list of required materials and their approximate costs

- Detailed, illustrated installation instructions
- Configuration guidance for various platforms
- Creative ideas for expanding and customizing the project
- Common pitfalls and how to avoid them

The Projects Ahead

To give you a taste of what's to come, here are some of the projects we'll explore:

- **Creating a robust smart home network** – The often-overlooked foundation of any successful smart home
- **Smart lighting on any budget** – From simple plug-in solutions to whole-home lighting automation
- **Climate control optimization** – Beyond basic programmable thermostats to truly intelligent environmental systems
- **DIY security implementations** – Building comprehensive security with cameras, sensors, and intelligent alerts
- **Entertainment automation** – Creating seamless media experiences throughout your home
- **Voice control integration** – Maximizing the usefulness of voice assistants while maintaining privacy
- **Custom sensor projects** – Building specialized sensors for unique needs, from water leak detection to air quality monitoring

- **Automation routines** – Creating sophisticated sequences that make your home truly responsive
- **Data visualization** – Gaining insights from your smart home data to further optimize your environment

Your Smart Home Journey

As you embark on this journey, remember that the perfect smart home isn't built in a day. The most successful implementations grow organically, with each addition building upon a foundation of knowledge and experience.

This book isn't just about following instructions to install devices—it's about developing a mindset and skillset that empowers you to create a home environment that genuinely enhances your daily life. The projects and principles we'll explore are designed to spark your creativity and inspire innovations unique to your lifestyle.

Whether your primary motivation is convenience, energy efficiency, security, accessibility, or simply the satisfaction of creating something remarkable, the path ahead offers rich rewards. The smart home you build will be more than a collection of devices—it will be a personalized environment that anticipates needs, removes friction from daily tasks, and provides peace of mind.

So let's begin this journey together, transforming the

place you live into a home that works intelligently for you. Welcome to the world of DIY home automation— where technology meets imagination to create living spaces that once existed only in our dreams.

Chapter 1: Getting Started with Home Automation

What is Home Automation?

Home automation refers to the automatic control and programming of household devices, appliances, and systems to perform actions with minimal human intervention. Unlike traditional homes where each device functions independently and requires manual operation, automated homes feature interconnected devices that communicate with each other and respond to programmed conditions, user preferences, or environmental changes.

At its core, home automation transforms passive elements of your living space into active participants in creating a more comfortable, efficient, and secure environment. While the concept might sound futuristic, today's home automation technology has reached a level of accessibility that makes it practical for virtually any homeowner regardless of technical expertise.

The scope of home automation extends to nearly every aspect of residential life:

- **Lighting**: From simple scheduling to context-aware illumination that responds to occupancy, time of day, and ambient conditions
- **Climate control**: Intelligent management of heating, cooling, humidity, and ventilation for optimal comfort and efficiency
- **Security**: Integrated monitoring, access control, and alert systems that provide comprehensive protection
- **Entertainment**: Seamless audio and video experiences that follow you throughout your home
- **Appliances**: Smart kitchen devices, laundry equipment, and other household tools that optimize their operations
- **Energy management**: Monitoring and control systems that reduce waste and lower utility bills
- **Convenience features**: Automated routines that handle repetitive tasks and anticipate needs

Modern home automation diverges significantly from earlier systems in several important ways. While sophisticated automation has been available to luxury homeowners for decades, those systems typically required professional installation, proprietary hardware, and substantial investments. Today's technology leverages standard wireless protocols, cloud computing, and smartphone integration to deliver similar or superior capabilities at a fraction of the cost and complexity.

Perhaps most importantly, contemporary home

automation emphasizes flexibility and user control. Rather than locking you into rigid, pre-programmed behaviors, modern systems empower you to easily modify, expand, and customize your automation to suit your evolving needs and preferences.

Basic Concepts: Sensors, Controllers, Smart Devices

To build an effective smart home, it's essential to understand the fundamental components that make automation possible. While the specific technologies may vary, virtually all home automation systems incorporate three key elements: sensors, controllers, and smart devices.

Sensors: The Eyes and Ears of Your Smart Home

Sensors gather information about the environment, serving as the input mechanism for your automation system. Without sensors, smart homes would be blind and deaf, unable to respond to changing conditions or detect when action is needed. Common sensors include:

- **Motion sensors**: Detect movement within a specified area, triggering lighting, security alerts, or other responses
- **Door/window sensors**: Monitor the open/closed status of entries, essential for both security and climate control
- **Temperature sensors**: Measure ambient temperatures to inform heating and cooling decisions

- **Humidity sensors**: Track moisture levels in the air, important for comfort and preventing mold issues
- **Light sensors**: Detect ambient brightness, enabling automation based on natural light conditions
- **Occupancy sensors**: More sophisticated than motion sensors, these can determine if a space is actively being used
- **Water leak sensors**: Placed near potential problem areas to provide early warning of water damage
- **Smoke/CO detectors**: Critical safety sensors that can integrate with broader home systems
- **Air quality sensors**: Monitor pollutants, particulates, and VOCs for health and comfort optimization

Each sensor type creates opportunities for specific automation scenarios. For example, a motion sensor in a hallway might trigger lights to illuminate your path at night, while that same sensor might arm your security system when integrated with time-of-day awareness.

Controllers: The Brain of Your Smart Home

If sensors are the sensory organs of your smart home, controllers represent the brain. These devices process information from sensors, apply programmed logic, and issue commands to smart devices. Controllers take many forms:

- **Dedicated hubs**: Purpose-built devices that serve as central coordination points (e.g., Samsung SmartThings, Hubitat Elevation)
- **Voice assistants**: Smart speakers that combine voice control with automation capabilities (e.g., Amazon Echo, Google Nest)
- **Software controllers**: Applications running on computers, smartphones, or cloud services
- **Specialized controllers**: Devices focused on specific systems like security or climate control

The controller layer is where the "intelligence" in your smart home resides. Modern controllers employ various approaches to decision-making:

- **Rule-based logic**: Simple if-then scenarios (e.g., "If motion is detected and it's after sunset, turn on the lights")
- **Schedule-based automation**: Actions that occur at specific times or intervals
- **Scene-based control**: Predefined configurations that can be activated as a group
- **Contextual awareness**: More sophisticated programming that considers multiple factors simultaneously
- **Machine learning**: Advanced systems that adjust their behavior based on observed patterns

For DIY smart home builders, the choice of controller often determines the overall architecture of your system and influences which devices you can integrate effectively.

Smart Devices: The Muscle of Your Smart Home

Smart devices execute the actions in your automation system, serving as the output mechanism that creates tangible changes in your environment. These connected devices receive commands from controllers and implement the desired effects:

- **Smart bulbs and switches**: Control lighting throughout your home
- **Smart thermostats**: Manage heating and cooling systems
- **Smart locks**: Secure and control access to your home
- **Smart speakers**: Provide audio output and often voice control
- **Smart plugs/outlets**: Control power to conventional appliances
- **Smart appliances**: Refrigerators, ovens, washers, and other household equipment with built-in connectivity
- **Smart blinds/shades**: Automate natural light and privacy control
- **Smart irrigation systems**: Intelligent watering for lawns and gardens
- **Smart entertainment systems**: TVs, audio equipment, and media streamers with network capabilities

Unlike conventional household devices that operate independently, smart devices are distinguished by three key capabilities:

1. **Connectivity**: The ability to communicate with controllers and other devices
2. **Programmability**: Support for automated control beyond simple manual operation
3. **State reporting**: The capacity to report their current status to the broader system

The distinction between "**smart**" and "**connected**" devices is worth noting. While all smart devices are connected, not all connected devices are truly smart. Some products offer remote control through smartphone apps but lack the ability to integrate with broader automation systems or respond to environmental conditions.

The Interplay Between Components

A successful home automation system depends on the seamless interaction between sensors, controllers, and smart devices. Consider a simple example of arriving home in the evening:

1. **Sensor input**: Your smartphone's GPS (acting as a location sensor) detects you're approaching home
2. **Controller processing**: Your automation hub recognizes this trigger and checks additional context (time of day, sunset status)
3. **Device output**: Smart locks disengage, entryway lights activate at appropriate brightness, thermostat adjusts to occupied settings, and perhaps your favorite music begins playing

This harmonious interaction between components creates experiences that feel magical—your home responding to your needs without explicit commands. As your system grows in sophistication, these interactions become increasingly seamless and intuitive.

Choosing the Right Devices: Smart Bulbs, Locks, Thermostats

With thousands of smart home products on the market, selecting the right devices for your needs can be overwhelming. This section will help you navigate the essential categories, understanding the options, benefits, and limitations of each.

Smart Lighting: Illuminating Possibilities

Smart lighting represents one of the most accessible and immediately rewarding entry points into home automation. Options include:

Smart Bulbs:

- **Pros**: Easiest installation (simply replace existing bulbs), no wiring required, often include color-changing capabilities
- **Cons**: Relatively expensive per bulb, require power at all times (switches must remain on), may need replacement when light technology advances
- **Best for**: Renters, those seeking color-changing options, targeted deployment in specific fixtures

Smart Switches:

- **Pros**: Control existing fixtures and bulbs, maintain traditional wall control, often more cost-effective for controlling multiple bulbs
- **Cons**: Require installation with wiring knowledge, most need neutral wires, less likely to offer color-changing features
- **Best for**: Homeowners committed to long-term automation, controlling multiple bulbs with one device

Smart Plugs with Lamps:

- **Pros**: No wiring required, can use with favorite existing lamps, very flexible placement
- **Cons**: Only works for plug-in lighting, requires more devices, may have limited control options
- **Best for**: Table and floor lamps, temporary solutions, renters

When evaluating smart lighting, consider these factors:

- **Protocol compatibility**: Ensure the products work with your chosen ecosystem
- **Brightness capabilities**: Check lumen output and color temperature ranges
- **Power failure behavior**: How do they respond when power is restored?
- **Dimming performance**: Some options flicker or buzz when dimmed

- **Hub requirements**: Some require dedicated bridges or gateways

For beginners, we recommend starting with a few strategic smart bulbs in frequently used areas before expanding to more comprehensive solutions.

Smart Locks: Securing Access

Smart locks transform one of your home's most fundamental security elements, offering convenience without compromising protection:

Retrofit Smart Locks:

- **Pros**: Install over existing deadbolts, preserving exterior appearance, easier installation
- **Cons**: Bulky interior appearance, may not fit all door preparations
- **Best for**: Renters (with permission), quick deployment, those who want to maintain existing keying

Complete Smart Lock Systems:

- **Pros**: Fully integrated design, often sleeker appearance, may offer advanced features
- **Cons**: Requires full lock replacement, typically more expensive
- **Best for**: Homeowners, new construction, those wanting a unified look

Smart Lock Features to Consider:

- **Access methods**: Keypad, fingerprint, proximity, app control, physical key backup
- **Remote control capabilities**: Can you lock/unlock from anywhere, or only when nearby?
- **Guest access**: Temporary codes for visitors, service personnel
- **Activity logging**: Records of when the lock was used and by whom
- **Auto-lock features**: Automatically secure the door after entry or on a schedule
- **Battery life**: How often you'll need to replace batteries
- **Mechanical key override**: Essential for power failures

Smart locks represent a significant security element, so prioritize reliability and security features over novelty functions. Look for products with strong encryption and data protection practices.

Smart Thermostats: Climate Intelligence

Smart thermostats offer some of the most tangible benefits in home automation, potentially paying for themselves through energy savings:

Learning Thermostats:

- **Pros**: Adapt to your patterns automatically, typically user-friendly
- **Cons**: Generally more expensive, may make assumptions that require correction

- **Best for**: Households with regular schedules, those who prefer minimal programming

Programmable Smart Thermostats:

- **Pros**: Usually more affordable, offer precise control over schedules
- **Cons**: Require more initial setup, less adaptive to changing patterns
- **Best for**: Those who prefer explicit control, variable occupancy homes

Advanced Climate Systems:

- **Pros**: Support for multi-zone control, integration with additional sensors, wider HVAC compatibility
- **Cons**: Highest cost, more complex setup, may require professional installation
- **Best for**: Larger homes, complex heating/cooling systems, comprehensive automation

Key Thermostat Considerations:

- **HVAC system compatibility**: Verify the thermostat works with your specific system
- **C-wire requirements**: Many smart thermostats need a common wire for power
- **Sensor capabilities**: Remote temperature sensors improve comfort in larger homes
- **Energy monitoring**: Usage tracking helps identify savings opportunities

- **Integration depth**: How well it works with other smart home elements
- **Voice control support**: Compatibility with your preferred assistant
- **Screen and interface design**: You'll interact with this device regularly

Smart thermostats often deliver the most significant ROI among smart home devices, making them an excellent starting point for automation beginners.

Smart Home Systems: Google Assistant, Amazon Alexa, Apple HomeKit

The backbone of any effective smart home is the ecosystem or platform that connects and coordinates your devices. While you can mix components from different systems, focusing on a primary ecosystem simplifies integration and creates more reliable automation. Let's explore the major platforms and their distinctive characteristics.

Amazon Alexa: Voice-First Versatility

Amazon's Alexa ecosystem has evolved from simple voice commands to a comprehensive smart home platform:

Strengths:

- Widest device compatibility with thousands of supported products

- Extensive voice control capabilities with natural language processing
- Broad range of Echo devices at various price points
- Routines feature allows creating custom automation sequences
- Strong multimedia integration (music, video, communications)

Limitations:

- Less intuitive visual interface for device management
- Privacy concerns regarding voice recording and processing
- Requires separate hub for certain device types (Zigbee, Z-Wave)
- Automation capabilities less sophisticated than specialized platforms

Best for: Users who prioritize voice control, those with existing Echo devices, households seeking broad compatibility with budget-friendly devices.

Google Assistant: Integration and Intelligence

Google's approach leverages their strengths in search and AI for a smart home platform centered around the Google Home app and Nest devices:

Strengths:

- Superior natural language processing and question answering
- Tight integration with Google services (Calendar, Maps, etc.)
- Elegant user interface through the Google Home app
- Strong support for multimedia control and content discovery
- Improving contextual awareness across devices

Limitations:

- Fewer compatible devices than Alexa ecosystem
- More limited automation capabilities without additional systems
- Changing platform strategies have caused confusion
- Privacy considerations similar to other voice-first systems

Best for: Android users, households integrated with Google services, those who value conversational interactions and information retrieval.

Apple HomeKit: Privacy and Polish

Apple's smart home platform emphasizes security, privacy, and tight integration with the iOS ecosystem:

Strengths:

- Industry-leading privacy protections and local processing

- Exceptionally polished user interface through the Home app
- Reliable performance with less troubleshooting required
- Seamless integration with Apple devices and services
- Strong security standards for certified devices

Limitations:

- Significantly fewer compatible devices due to strict certification
- Higher average price point for supported products
- Requires Apple devices for full functionality
- More limited voice control through Siri compared to competitors

Best for: Apple ecosystem users, privacy-conscious consumers, those who value reliability and simplicity over extensive device options.

Hub-Based Systems: SmartThings, Hubitat, Home Assistant

Beyond the big three consumer platforms, several hub-centered systems offer more advanced capabilities:

Samsung SmartThings:

- Bridges the gap between consumer-friendly and power-user options

- Supports numerous protocols including Zigbee and Z-Wave
- Offers local processing with cloud backup
- Provides more sophisticated automation rules

Hubitat Elevation:

- Focuses on local processing without cloud dependency
- Offers extremely low latency for automation
- Supports extensive device types through multiple protocols
- Provides powerful rule creation for advanced users

Home Assistant:

- Open-source platform with unmatched flexibility
- Runs on various hardware from Raspberry Pi to dedicated servers
- Supports the broadest range of devices and integrations
- Offers the most powerful automation capabilities

These specialized platforms typically require more technical knowledge but deliver significantly more capability for advanced automation scenarios.

Making Your Ecosystem Choice

When selecting your primary smart home ecosystem, consider these factors:

1. **Existing devices**: Which smartphones, tablets, or speakers do you already own?
2. **Voice assistant preference**: Which voice assistant do you find most natural to use?
3. **Privacy priorities**: How important is local processing versus cloud-based systems?
4. **Technical comfort level**: Are you seeking simplicity or power and customization?
5. **Specific device needs**: Which platform supports the particular devices you want?

For beginners, we recommend starting with the ecosystem that aligns with your current technology usage. If you're an iPhone user, HomeKit offers the most seamless experience. Android users will find Google Assistant integration more natural, while those prioritizing wide device compatibility might prefer Alexa.

Remember that these ecosystems aren't entirely mutually exclusive. Many devices support multiple platforms simultaneously, and you can gradually transition between systems as your needs evolve.

Setting Up a Hub: Connecting Everything to One Control Center

While smartphone apps provide convenient control of individual smart devices, a dedicated hub creates a true automation system where devices work together intelligently. Hubs serve as the central nervous system of your smart home, enabling communication between devices that might otherwise remain isolated.

Types of Smart Home Hubs

The hub landscape includes several distinct approaches:

Standalone Hardware Hubs:

- Purpose-built devices dedicated to smart home management
- Examples: Samsung SmartThings Hub, Hubitat Elevation, Aeotec Smart Home Hub
- Typically support multiple wireless protocols directly
- Often provide more reliable automation than software-only solutions

Voice Assistant Devices with Hub Functionality:

- Smart speakers or displays that double as control centers
- Examples: Amazon Echo (4th gen), Google Nest Hub, Apple HomePod
- Combine voice control with basic hub capabilities
- Usually require additional hardware for certain protocols

Software Hubs:

- Applications that run on existing hardware (computers, servers)
- Examples: Home Assistant, Homebridge, openHAB
- Maximum flexibility and customization potential

- Require more technical knowledge to set up and maintain

Protocol-Specific Bridges:

- Connect specific device types to your broader system
- Examples: Philips Hue Bridge, Lutron Caseta Bridge, IKEA TRÅDFRI Gateway
- Optimize performance for their native devices
- Create potential points of failure in larger systems

Each approach offers different balances between simplicity, capability, reliability, and cost. Many advanced users eventually implement hybrid systems with multiple hub types working together.

Key Hub Selection Criteria

When evaluating hub options, consider these important factors:

Protocol Support: Different devices communicate using various wireless protocols:

- **Wi-Fi**: Familiar but power-hungry, ideal for always-powered devices
- **Bluetooth**: Limited range but energy-efficient for nearby control
- **Zigbee**: Low-power mesh network ideal for sensors and simple devices

- **Z-Wave**: Robust mesh network with excellent reliability and range
- **Thread/Matter**: Emerging standards promising better interoperability
- **Proprietary RF**: Used by some manufacturers for specific products

Your hub should support the protocols used by your current and planned devices.

Processing Location:

- **Cloud-dependent**: Requires internet connection, may have delays, typically easier to set up
- **Local processing**: Works without internet, faster response, more private, usually more complex

Automation Capabilities:

- **Basic triggers**: Simple if-then conditions
- **Scenes**: Grouped device states that activate together
- **Multi-condition rules**: More complex decision logic
- **Variables and mode awareness**: System can maintain state information
- **Custom code support**: Allows writing specialized functions

Reliability Considerations:

- **Offline functionality**: What happens during internet outages?

- **Backup options**: How configuration is preserved
- **Failure modes**: How devices behave when the hub is unavailable
- **Recovery procedures**: Steps required after system interruptions

Expansion Potential:

- **Device limits**: Maximum number of connected devices
- **Growth compatibility**: Support for future technologies
- **Ecosystem longevity**: Company track record and community support

Hub Setup and Configuration

While each hub system has its unique setup process, most follow these general steps:

1. **Physical placement**: Position your hub centrally in your home, ideally elevated and away from interference sources like microwaves or thick walls
2. **Network connection**: Connect the hub to your home network, preferably via ethernet for reliability (though many support Wi-Fi)
3. **Account creation**: Register with the manufacturer's service and download any required applications
4. **Device pairing**: Add your smart devices to the hub through its pairing process, which typically involves:

- Putting the hub in "discovery" or "pairing" mode
- Triggering a pairing action on the device (button press, power cycle)
- Naming and categorizing the device in your system
5. **Room/location assignment**: Organize devices by location for easier management
6. **Basic automation setup**: Create initial rules, scenes, or routines to establish core functionality
7. **Testing and verification**: Confirm that all devices respond correctly to both manual and automated controls
8. **Backup configuration**: Save your setup to prevent losing configuration during updates

For beginners, we recommend starting with consumer-friendly hubs like SmartThings or assistant-based options until you develop a better understanding of your specific needs and preferences.

Tools You'll Need: Basic Tools and Apps to Get Started

Building your smart home doesn't require extensive technical equipment, but having the right tools on hand will make the process significantly smoother. Let's explore the essential physical tools, software applications, and knowledge resources you'll need.

Physical Tools

Even for wireless smart home implementations, some basic tools are invaluable:

Essential Hand Tools:

- **Multi-bit screwdriver**: For mounting devices and accessing battery compartments
- **Wire strippers/cutters**: Essential for switch and outlet installations
- **Voltage tester**: Safety-critical for any electrical work
- **Measuring tape**: For planning device placement and wiring routes
- **Drill with bits**: For mounting sensors, cameras, and other equipment
- **Step ladder**: Safely reach lighting fixtures and high-mounted devices

Electrical Supplies:

- **Electrical tape**: Insulating connections and bundling wires
- **Wire nuts/connectors**: Joining electrical connections securely
- **Extra wire**: Low-voltage for sensors, 14-2 Romex for switches if needed
- **USB power adapters**: Powering hubs and USB-powered devices
- Extension cords/surge protectors: Temporary power during setup

Networking Equipment:

- **Ethernet cables**: Direct connections for hubs and critical devices

- **Wi-Fi analyzer app**: Identifying optimal channel and placement
- **Network labels**: Tracking which cables connect to which devices
- **Spare router/access point**: Testing network expansion if needed

Organization Tools:

- **Cable management supplies**: Preventing wire tangles and hazards
- **Device labels**: Tracking which device is which during complex setups
- **Small containers**: Keeping screws and small parts organized
- **Documentation notebook**: Recording settings, passwords, and configurations

Software Tools and Applications

The digital tools for your smart home project are equally important:

Essential Applications:

- **Manufacturer apps**: Each smart device typically requires its native app
- **Hub/ecosystem app**: Your primary control interface (SmartThings, Home, etc.)
- **Network scanner**: Identifying devices on your network
- **Password manager**: Securely storing the many credentials you'll create

- **Note-taking app**: Documenting your setup process and configuration

Helpful Utilities:

- **IFTTT (If This Then That)**: Creating simple cross-platform automations
- **Network speed test**: Verifying sufficient bandwidth
- **Floor plan software**: Planning device placement and coverage
- **Backup solutions**: Preserving configuration and automation rules

Advanced Tools (for technical users):

- **Terminal/command line**: Accessing advanced configuration options
- **MQTT clients**: Working with message-based device communication
- **Node-RED**: Visual programming for sophisticated automation
- **API testing tools**: Exploring device capabilities and integration options

Knowledge Resources

Perhaps the most valuable tools are information sources that guide your journey:

Documentation:

- **Device manuals**: Official operation and installation guides
- **Hub documentation**: Platform-specific setup and automation instructions
- **Home wiring guides**: Reference materials for electrical work
- **Network setup tutorials**: Resources for optimizing your connectivity

Community Resources:

- **Reddit communities**: r/homeautomation, r/smarthome, platform-specific subreddits
- **Manufacturer forums**: Official support and user discussions
- **Discord servers**: Real-time chat with other smart home enthusiasts
- **Local maker/DIY groups**: In-person assistance and inspiration

Learning Platforms:

- **YouTube channels**: Visual guides to installation and configuration
- **Online courses**: Structured learning for specific platforms
- **Blogs and websites**: Current trends and product reviews
- **Podcasts**: Discussions of technology and techniques

Smart Home Project Planning Tools

Before purchasing devices or installing anything, these planning approaches will save time and money:

1. Home Mapping:

- Create a simple floor plan noting:
    - Existing switch and outlet locations
    - Wi-Fi coverage areas and dead zones
    - Natural activity patterns and traffic flow
    - Problem areas you want to improve

2. Use Case Identification:

- Document specific scenarios you want to automate:
    - Morning and evening routines
    - Home arrival and departure sequences
    - Entertainment and relaxation settings
    - Security and monitoring needs

3. Prioritization Framework:

- Evaluate potential projects based on:
    - Implementation complexity
    - Potential benefit/impact
    - Cost considerations
    - Dependencies on other components

4. Phased Implementation Plan:

- Create a staged approach that:
    - Starts with fundamental infrastructure
    - Builds capabilities incrementally

- ○ Allows learning between phases
- ○ Preserves budget for adjustments

Getting Started: Your First Steps

With an understanding of the tools and resources available, here's a recommended sequence for beginning your smart home journey:

1. **Assess your network**: Ensure your Wi-Fi coverage and speed can support additional devices
2. **Select your primary ecosystem**: Choose the platform that best aligns with your priorities
3. **Start with standalone devices**: Begin with simple, high-impact products that work independently
4. **Add hub capabilities**: Introduce central coordination once you have several devices to manage
5. **Implement basic automation**: Create simple rules that demonstrate the potential
6. **Gather user feedback**: Learn how household members interact with the system
7. **Expand methodically**: Add capabilities based on actual usage patterns and needs

Remember that home automation is an iterative process. Your system will evolve as you learn more about the technology and discover which features truly enhance your daily life. The tools and resources outlined here provide the foundation for that journey of exploration and improvement.

Chapter 2: Wiring and Setting Up Smart Lights

Introduction to Smart Lighting

Smart lighting represents one of the most accessible and impactful entry points into home automation. Beyond the simple convenience of controlling lights from your phone, smart lighting systems can transform how you experience your living space, enhance security, reduce energy consumption, and create ambiance that responds to your needs and preferences.

The Evolution of Lighting Control

Home lighting has undergone several revolutionary changes throughout history. The transition from gas lamps to electric lights marked the first major shift, followed by the introduction of dimmer switches in the mid-20th century. The arrival of programmable timers and motion sensors in the 1980s and 1990s added basic automation capabilities. Today's smart lighting represents the next evolutionary leap—bringing intelligence, connectivity, and unprecedented control to home illumination.

Benefits of Smart Lighting

Smart lighting systems offer numerous advantages over conventional lighting:

Convenience and Control:

- Control lighting from anywhere via smartphone apps
- Voice command capabilities through virtual assistants
- Automated responses to schedules, sensors, and other triggers
- Granular brightness adjustment beyond basic on/off functionality

Energy Efficiency:

- Automated shutoff when rooms are unoccupied
- Dimming capabilities that reduce power consumption
- Scheduling to prevent lights from running unnecessarily
- Usage monitoring to identify optimization opportunities

Enhanced Security:

- Simulated occupancy when you're away from home
- Integration with security systems and cameras
- Motion-triggered illumination for deterrence
- Remote monitoring of light status

Mood and Ambiance:

- Color temperature adjustment to match time of day or activities
- Scene creation for different occasions or moods
- Dynamic lighting effects for entertainment or special events
- Gradual brightness transitions that feel natural

Health and Wellness:

- Circadian rhythm support through color temperature changes
- Gentle wake-up sequences instead of jarring alarms
- Reduced blue light exposure in evening hours
- Visual cues for notifications or reminders

Smart Lighting Components

Modern smart lighting systems typically include several key elements:

Smart Bulbs: Intelligent light sources that connect directly to networks or hubs. These range from basic white dimmable bulbs to sophisticated color-changing models with built-in effects.

Smart Switches and Dimmers: Wall-mounted replacements for traditional switches that control existing fixtures while adding smart capabilities.

Smart Plugs and Outlets: Devices that add intelligence to lamps and light fixtures without requiring new bulbs or wiring changes.

Motion and Occupancy Sensors: Devices that detect movement or presence to trigger lighting automatically.

Bridges and Hubs: Central connection points that coordinate multiple lights and integrate with broader home automation systems.

Controllers and Remotes: Physical interfaces that supplement app and voice control with convenient buttons and dials.

Smart Lighting Protocols

Smart lights communicate using various wireless protocols, each with distinct advantages:

Wi-Fi:

- Direct connection to your home network
- No hub required for basic functionality
- Typically higher power consumption
- May congest networks with many devices

Bluetooth:

- Simple direct connection to smartphones
- Limited range and device count
- Low power consumption
- Often challenging for whole-home solutions

Zigbee:

- Mesh network with excellent reliability

- Requires compatible hub/bridge
- Very low power consumption
- Extensive device compatibility

Z-Wave:

- Robust mesh network with good range
- Requires Z-Wave hub
- Operates on separate frequency from Wi-Fi
- Strong interoperability standards

Thread/Matter:

- Newer standard gaining adoption
- Designed for improved interoperability
- Combines benefits of existing protocols
- Forward-looking but still emerging

Your choice of protocol will influence your overall system architecture and expansion options. For beginners, we generally recommend starting with Wi-Fi for simplicity or Zigbee for reliability, depending on your technical comfort level.

Tools and Materials Needed

Proper preparation ensures your smart lighting project proceeds smoothly. The specific tools and materials required will vary based on your chosen approach, but this comprehensive list covers most common scenarios.

Essential Tools

Electrical Safety Tools:

- **Non-contact voltage tester**: Essential for verifying power is off before working on any wiring
- **Insulated screwdrivers**: Protect against accidental electrical contact
- **Circuit finder/breaker identifier**: Locate the correct breaker to disable
- **Electrical tape**: Insulate connections and bundle wires
- **Work gloves**: Protect hands during installation

Installation Tools:

- **Wire strippers/cutters**: Prepare wires for connection
- **Needle-nose pliers**: Manipulate wires in tight spaces
- **Level**: Ensure switches and fixtures are properly aligned
- **Measuring tape**: Position devices correctly
- **Drill and bits**: Mount brackets or create access for wiring
- **Stud finder**: Locate solid mounting points
- **Flashlight or headlamp**: Illuminate work areas, especially during power-off periods

Network Tools:

- **Smartphone or tablet**: Control setup applications
- **Wi-Fi analyzer app**: Verify signal strength in installation locations

- **Network credentials**: Have your Wi-Fi password readily available

Materials for Different Setup Types

For Smart Bulb Installation:

- Smart bulbs in appropriate base types (E26, BR30, etc.)
- Compatible hub/bridge (if required)
- Ethernet cable (for hub connection to router)
- Power strips or surge protectors

For Smart Switch Installation:

- Smart switches matching your existing switch type
- Wire nuts or lever connectors
- Electrical junction boxes (if expanding)
- Wall plates in appropriate style
- Extra 14/2 or 12/2 wire (if extending circuits)

For Smart Plug Setup:

- Smart plugs rated for your intended devices
- Tabletop or floor lamps with standard plugs
- Multi-outlet adapters (if needed)

For Comprehensive Systems:

- Motion/occupancy sensors
- Door/window sensors for trigger events
- Scene controllers or physical remotes

- Cable management supplies
- Mounting brackets or adhesive strips

Software and Account Requirements

Before beginning physical installation, ensure you have:

- Downloaded manufacturer apps for your devices
- Created accounts with relevant services
- Updated your smartphone operating system
- Verified hub/bridge firmware is current
- Documented your network name and password
- Familiarized yourself with user manuals

Safety Equipment

Smart lighting installation often involves electrical work, requiring proper safety measures:

- **Rubber-soled shoes**: Provide electrical insulation
- **Safety glasses**: Protect eyes from debris
- **First aid kit**: Address minor injuries quickly
- **Fire extinguisher**: Precaution for any electrical work
- **Proper lighting**: Illuminate work areas clearly

Optional Specialized Tools

For more advanced installations, consider having access to:

- **Multimeter**: Test voltage and continuity

- **Fish tape**: Route wires through walls
- Drywall repair supplies: Patch access holes
- **Cable tracer**: Identify wires in walls
- **Voltage stabilizer**: Protect sensitive electronics

Having these tools and materials organized before beginning will significantly reduce frustration and improvisation during your smart lighting installation.

Step-by-Step Instructions: How to Wire and Install Smart Bulbs

While smart bulbs are often considered the simplest entry point to smart lighting, proper installation ensures optimal performance and reliability. This section provides detailed guidance for installing different types of smart lighting solutions.

Smart Bulb Installation Process

1. Preparation and Planning:

- Identify fixtures for smart bulb installation
- Verify bulb compatibility (base type, shape, wattage limitations)
- Ensure fixtures will remain powered (switches must stay on)
- Check Wi-Fi/network coverage in installation locations
- Download required manufacturer apps

2. Initial Device Setup:

- Unpack bulbs and hub/bridge (if applicable)
- Connect hub to power and your router via ethernet
- Install fresh batteries in remotes or sensors
- Power on the hub and wait for status indicators
- Complete hub registration through manufacturer app

3. Installing the Smart Bulbs:

- Turn off power to the fixture at the switch
- Remove existing bulb (allow to cool if recently used)
- Insert smart bulb, ensuring secure but not overtight fit
- Restore power to the fixture
- Leave switch in the ON position

4. Connecting Bulbs to Your System:

- Open manufacturer app on your smartphone
- Follow app-specific discovery process (typically "Add Device")
- Place phone near the bulb during pairing
- Confirm successful connection when bulb flashes or changes color
- Name the bulb clearly (e.g., "Living Room Table Lamp")

5. Basic Configuration:

- Test on/off functionality through the app

- Adjust brightness levels to verify dimming capability
- Set default power-on behavior (brightness, color)
- Organize bulbs into rooms or zones
- Create basic scenes (e.g., "Reading," "Movie Night")

6. Integration with Voice Assistants:

- Link your lighting system to your preferred voice assistant
- Discover devices through assistant settings
- Test voice commands for basic control
- Create assistant routines that include lighting

Wiring Smart Switches (More Advanced)

For those looking to replace wall switches with smart alternatives, the process requires basic electrical knowledge:

1. Safety Preparation:

- Turn off power at the circuit breaker
- Verify power is off using voltage tester
- Take a photo of existing wiring for reference
- Identify wire types (line, load, neutral, ground)

2. Removing Existing Switch:

- Remove wall plate and mounting screws
- Pull switch assembly from the wall box

- Disconnect wires, labeling if needed
- Note wire colors and connections

3. Examining Wiring Configuration:

- Identify neutral wire (typically white)
- Locate line wire (brings power to switch)
- Find load wire (goes to light fixture)
- Verify ground wire presence (typically bare copper or green)

4. Special Considerations for Smart Switches:

- Most smart switches require a neutral wire
- If neutral is absent, consider specific no-neutral models
- For three-way circuits (controlled from multiple locations), ensure compatible switch type
- Verify box depth accommodates larger smart switch housing

5. Connecting the Smart Switch:

- Connect ground wire to switch's green terminal
- Attach neutral wire to switch's neutral terminal
- Connect line (power) wire to "Line" or "L" terminal
- Attach load wire (to fixture) to "Load" or light icon terminal
- For travelers in three-way setups, follow manufacturer instructions

6. Finalizing Installation:

- Carefully fold wires back into box
- Mount switch using provided screws
- Attach faceplate
- Restore power at breaker
- Test manual switch operation before proceeding to smart setup

7. Connecting to Smart System:

- Follow manufacturer app instructions for adding switches
- Configure switch settings (LED indicator, behavior when pressed)
- Add to appropriate rooms/groups in your system
- Test automated control and schedules

Smart Plug Installation (Simplest Option)

For lamps and non-hardwired lighting, smart plugs offer the fastest path to automation:

1. Preparation:

- Choose appropriate lamp or light fixture
- Verify power ratings (don't exceed plug's maximum wattage)
- Ensure conventional switch on lamp is accessible
- Position where both Wi-Fi signal and physical access are good

2. Physical Setup:

- Insert smart plug into wall outlet

- Connect lamp to smart plug
- Turn lamp's physical switch to ON position
- Check that indicator lights on smart plug are visible

3. Connection Process:

- Open manufacturer's app
- Select "Add Device" or similar option
- Follow pairing instructions (may involve pressing button on plug)
- Wait for confirmation of successful connection
- Name the plug descriptively (e.g., "Bedroom Reading Lamp")

4. Basic Configuration:

- Test on/off functionality
- Set up any specific features (power monitoring, etc.)
- Add to appropriate room groups
- Create initial automation rules if desired

For any installation type, keeping detailed notes of your setup process, including device names, locations, and any special configurations, will prove invaluable for future maintenance and troubleshooting.

DIY Project: Set Up a Smart Lighting System with a Hub

Creating a comprehensive smart lighting system that functions as an integrated whole requires thoughtful planning and implementation. This DIY project walks you through establishing a hub-based system that can grow with your needs.

Project Goal

Transform standard lighting throughout a living space into an intelligent, responsive system that adapts to occupancy, time of day, and user preferences.

Project Components

Core System Elements:

- Central lighting hub/bridge
- 4-6 smart bulbs for main living areas
- 1-2 smart switches for frequently used fixtures
- Motion sensor for entryway or hallway
- Smart button or remote for physical control

Step 1: System Planning

Before purchasing components, create a lighting plan:

- Map your home's floor plan
- Mark existing light fixtures and switches
- Identify high-traffic areas and key activity zones
- Determine which control method is best for each location
- Consider natural light patterns throughout the day
- Note special requirements (dimming, color changing, etc.)

Step 2: Hub Installation and Configuration

The hub serves as the foundation of your system:

1. Position hub centrally in your home for optimal coverage
2. Connect hub to power supply
3. Link hub to your router via ethernet cable
4. Download manufacturer's app and create account
5. Follow app instructions to initialize the hub
6. Check for and apply any available firmware updates
7. Configure basic hub settings (name, location, etc.)

Step 3: Adding Primary Lighting Elements

Begin with the most frequently used areas:

1. Install smart bulbs in main living space fixtures
2. Add each bulb to your hub following manufacturer instructions
3. Name bulbs based on location for easy identification
4. Test basic control of each bulb through the app
5. Create logical groups (e.g., "Living Room," "Kitchen")
6. Establish basic scenes (e.g., "Bright," "Relaxing," "Movie")

Step 4: Installing and Configuring Smart Switches

For fixtures with multiple bulbs, smart switches are often more practical:

1. Follow switch wiring instructions (ensure power is off)
2. Complete physical installation and restore power
3. Add switch to your hub system
4. Test manual and app control functionality
5. Link switch to appropriate groups in your system
6. Configure tap behaviors (single press, double press, etc.)

Step 5: Sensor Integration

Add responsiveness with occupancy detection:

1. Mount motion/presence sensor in strategic location
    o Entryway for arrival lighting
    o Hallway for nighttime navigation
    o Bathroom for hands-free control
2. Add sensor to your hub system
3. Configure detection sensitivity and timeout duration
4. Create basic automation rule:
    o Trigger: Motion detected
    o Condition: After sunset (or low light level)
    o Action: Turn on specified lights at 40% brightness
    o Additional: Turn off after 5 minutes of no motion

Step 6: Physical Control Implementation

Add convenient manual controls:

1. Install wireless remote or button controller
2. Add controller to your hub system
3. Program button functions:
   - Single press: Toggle lights on/off
   - Double press: Activate specific scene
   - Long press: All lights off
4. Mount in accessible location or use as portable remote

Step 7: Voice Assistant Integration

Connect your system to voice control:

1. In hub app, locate integration settings
2. Select your preferred assistant (Alexa, Google, etc.)
3. Link accounts following assistant's instructions
4. Discover devices through assistant app
5. Test basic voice commands
6. Create custom phrases for specific scenes

Step 8: Creating Advanced Automation

Build intelligence into your system:

1. Morning routine:
   - Trigger: Specific time or first motion after 6 AM
   - Action: Gradually increase brightness with warmer color
   - Condition: Only on weekdays

2. Evening transition:
   - Trigger: Sunset or specific time
   - Action: Adjust lights to warmer temperature and medium brightness
   - Optional: Different scenes for different areas
3. Away-from-home security:
   - Trigger: Home/Away status change
   - Action: Simulate occupancy with randomized lighting
   - Condition: Only during evening hours
4. Movie time integration:
   - Trigger: Smart remote button or voice command
   - Action: Dim living room lights, turn off hallway
   - Optional: Integration with TV or media system

Project Extensions

Once your basic system is operational, consider these enhancements:

- Expand to additional rooms following the same methodology
- Add light strips for accent lighting in entertainment areas
- Integrate with additional sensors (door/window, light level)
- Connect with other smart home systems (security, climate)

- Implement advanced rules based on multiple conditions
- Create seasonal lighting scenes and holiday displays

This modular approach allows you to build your system incrementally, ensuring each component works properly before expanding. Document your setup process, including device names, locations, and automation rules, to simplify future modifications and troubleshooting.

Troubleshooting Common Issues

Even well-planned smart lighting systems occasionally encounter challenges. This section addresses the most frequent problems and provides practical solutions.

Connectivity Problems

Issue: Bulbs or Switches Won't Connect to Hub

- **Solution 1**: Verify the device is within range of your hub (typically 30-50 feet)
- **Solution 2**: Confirm hub firmware is updated to latest version
- **Solution 3**: Reset the device according to manufacturer instructions
- **Solution 4**: Add a repeater device to extend network range
- **Solution 5**: Check for interference from other electronics

Issue: Devices Disconnect Frequently

- **Solution 1**: Move hub to more central location
- **Solution 2**: Verify you haven't exceeded maximum device count
- **Solution 3**: Check for Wi-Fi channel congestion and adjust router settings
- **Solution 4**: Add more repeater devices to strengthen mesh network
- **Solution 5**: Ensure hub has stable power supply (not on switched outlet)

Issue: Hub Cannot Connect to Internet

- **Solution 1**: Verify router is functioning properly
- **Solution 2**: Check ethernet cable connection
- **Solution 3**: Restart hub and router
- **Solution 4**: Confirm router hasn't blocked hub's MAC address
- **Solution 5**: Try alternative ethernet port on router

Physical Installation Issues

Issue: Smart Switch Has No Power

- **Solution 1**: Verify breaker is turned on
- **Solution 2**: Check wire connections for looseness
- **Solution 3**: Confirm line and load wires aren't reversed
- **Solution 4**: Test for voltage at switch location
- **Solution 5**: Ensure neutral wire is properly connected if required

Issue: Smart Bulb Flickers

- **Solution 1**: Check for loose connection in socket
- **Solution 2**: Verify bulb is compatible with fixture
- **Solution 3**: Test if dimmer switch is causing interference
- **Solution 4**: Try bulb in different fixture to isolate problem
- **Solution 5**: Check for power quality issues in your home

Issue: Motion Sensor Fails to Trigger

- **Solution 1**: Adjust sensitivity settings
- **Solution 2**: Reposition to improve coverage area
- **Solution 3**: Replace batteries if battery-powered
- **Solution 4**: Clean sensor lens
- **Solution 5**: Check for obstructions or interference sources

Software and Control Problems

Issue: App Cannot Find Devices

- **Solution 1**: Verify smartphone is on same network as hub
- **Solution 2**: Force close and restart the app
- **Solution 3**: Log out and log back into your account
- **Solution 4**: Check for app updates
- **Solution 5**: Clear app cache or reinstall if persistent

Issue: Automations Don't Execute Reliably

- **Solution 1**: Simplify rule conditions to isolate problem
- **Solution 2**: Check device status in app matches actual state
- **Solution 3**: Verify time zone settings are correct
- **Solution 4**: Review automation logic for conflicts
- **Solution 5**: Rebuild automation from scratch

Issue: Voice Control Inconsistent

- **Solution 1**: Refresh device connections in assistant app
- **Solution 2**: Check naming conventions for confusion
- **Solution 3**: Verify account linking is current
- **Solution 4**: Test assistant with simple commands first
- **Solution 5**: Re-link hub service with assistant

System Performance Issues

Issue: Significant Response Lag

- **Solution 1**: Reduce network congestion from other devices
- **Solution 2**: Check for firmware updates
- **Solution 3**: Verify hub isn't overloaded with devices
- **Solution 4**: Prioritize hub traffic on your router if possible

- **Solution 5**: Consider system architecture changes for larger installations

Issue: Scenes Activate Incompletely

- **Solution 1**: Simplify scene to identify problematic device
- **Solution 2**: Check individual device connectivity
- **Solution 3**: Recreate scene with fewer simultaneous changes
- **Solution 4**: Verify scene hasn't been modified accidentally
- **Solution 5**: Implement scene through different control method

Diagnostic Approaches

When troubleshooting persistent issues, follow this methodical process:

1. Isolate the problem:
   - Is it affecting one device or many?
   - Is it constant or intermittent?
   - Did it begin after a specific change or update?
2. Check the basics:
   - Power supply stability
   - Network connectivity
   - Physical installation integrity
   - Recent system changes
3. Consult documentation:
   - Review manufacturer troubleshooting guides

- ○ Check for known issues with your specific devices
- ○ Look for firmware update notes
4. Community resources:
   - ○ Search user forums for similar problems
   - ○ Check online communities for solutions
   - ○ Review product reviews for common complaints
5. Systematic testing:
   - ○ Test minimal configuration to establish baseline
   - ○ Add complexity incrementally to identify breaking point
   - ○ Document results of each test

Most smart lighting issues stem from either connectivity problems, physical installation errors, or software configuration mistakes. By approaching troubleshooting methodically, you can usually identify and resolve the root cause without needing to replace equipment.

Advanced Option: Automated Lighting Schedules

Once your basic smart lighting system is operational, implementing sophisticated automated schedules can dramatically enhance convenience, energy efficiency, and home security. This section explores advanced scheduling techniques that go beyond simple timers.

Beyond Basic Timers

Traditional lighting timers follow rigid schedules

regardless of conditions. Smart lighting automation offers far more flexibility:

Context-Aware Scheduling:

- Adjusts based on sunrise/sunset times throughout the year
- Responds to actual home occupancy rather than fixed times
- Adapts to weekend vs. weekday patterns
- Considers weather conditions and natural light levels

Adaptive Learning:

- Observes usage patterns over time
- Suggests optimizations based on actual behavior
- Refines schedules to match lifestyle changes
- Provides energy usage insights for further improvement

Creating Circadian Lighting Schedules

Our bodies respond naturally to changing light conditions throughout the day. Smart lighting can support healthy circadian rhythms:

Morning Transition (6:00-9:00 AM):

1. Begin with warm light (2700K) at 10% brightness
2. Gradually increase to cooler color temperature (4000K)

3. Reach full brightness by usual wakeup time
4. Maintain cool, bright light during morning activities

Daytime Setting (9:00 AM-5:00 PM):

1. Maintain cooler color temperature (4000-5000K)
2. Adjust brightness based on natural light sensing
3. Support alertness and productivity
4. Complement rather than compete with daylight

Evening Transition (5:00-9:00 PM):

1. Gradually shift to warmer color (3000K)
2. Reduce brightness levels
3. Create distinct lighting zones for different activities
4. Support transition to relaxation time

Nighttime Setting (9:00 PM-6:00 AM):

1. Use very warm light (2200-2700K)
2. Minimize blue light exposure
3. Keep brightness low in hallways and bathrooms
4. Implement gentle night light functionality

To create this schedule:

1. Check if your hub system has built-in circadian rhythm features
2. If not, create time-based automations for each transition period

3. Specify color temperature and brightness levels for each state
4. Add conditions for occupancy to prevent wasted energy
5. Consider separate weekend schedules based on different wake times

Security-Focused Scheduling

Smart lighting serves as an effective security tool when properly automated:

Vacation Mode Setup:

1. Create randomized on/off patterns that mimic occupancy
2. Vary which lights activate rather than fixed sequences
3. Focus on typically used areas visible from outside
4. Include occasional brief bathroom or kitchen light activations
5. Complement with randomized TV simulator or media playback

Predictive Away Lighting:

1. Use geofencing to detect when household members leave
2. Activate normal usage patterns based on historical data
3. Include gradual changes throughout the evening

4. Implement proper shut-down sequence at typical bedtime

Alarm Integration:

1. Connect lighting system with security system if available
2. Program all lights to activate during alarm events
3. Create attention-getting effects (flashing) for specific alerts
4. Ensure critical pathway illumination during emergencies

Perimeter Illumination Strategy:

1. Schedule exterior lighting based on sunset/sunrise
2. Add motion sensitivity during nighttime hours
3. Create "light escort" that follows movement around property
4. Maintain minimum illumination at potential entry points

Energy Optimization Scheduling

Strategic lighting automation can significantly reduce energy consumption:

Occupancy-Based Controls:

1. Install occupancy sensors in frequently trafficked areas

2. Configure automatic shutoff after 5-15 minutes of no movement
3. Implement reduced brightness during detected presence
4. Override functionality for special occasions

Daylight Harvesting:

1. Use light level sensors or time-based approximation
2. Automatically dim artificial lighting when natural light is sufficient
3. Create graduated response based on measured light levels
4. Prioritize natural light in regularly occupied spaces

Peak Usage Avoidance:

1. Research your utility's peak rate hours
2. Minimize discretionary lighting during high-rate periods
3. Pre-illuminate spaces just before peak periods if needed
4. Integrate with energy monitoring systems if available

Usage Analysis and Adaptation:

1. Review energy consumption data from smart bulbs/switches
2. Identify opportunities for schedule optimization

3. Implement automated "energy saving mode" during low occupancy
4. Create alerts for unusual energy usage patterns

Implementing Advanced Schedules

To set up sophisticated scheduling, leverage these techniques:

1. Conditional Logic Implementation:

- Use IF-THEN-ELSE structures in automation
- Combine multiple conditions (time, occupancy, light level)
- Create state variables to track system mode
- Implement priority overrides for special situations

2. Scene Sequencing:

- Define distinct scenes for different times of day
- Create smooth transitions between scenes
- Schedule scene activation on appropriate triggers
- Allow manual overrides that reset after a specific duration

3. API and Service Integration:

- Connect with weather services for cloud/sun awareness
- Use calendar integration for special event lighting

- Link with sleep tracking for personalized schedules
- Incorporate traffic information for arrival prediction

4. Multi-System Coordination:

- Synchronize lighting with HVAC schedules
- Coordinate with the entertainment system status
- Integrate with security system modes
- Connect with smart blinds/shades for complete light management

5. User Preference Layers:

- Create user-specific lighting preferences
- Implement a priority system for conflicting preferences
- Allow temporary schedule suspensions
- Provide easy restoration of standard schedules

Measuring and Refining Your System

The most effective automated lighting systems continuously improve through:

Data Collection:

- Track actual usage patterns versus scheduled activities
- Monitor energy consumption by fixture and room
- Record manual overrides and adjustments

- Note correlation with external factors (weather, seasons)

Performance Analysis:

- Identify frequently overridden automations
- Calculate energy savings from occupancy detection
- Measure response times and system reliability
- Evaluate user satisfaction with different scenes

Iterative Improvement:

- Make small adjustments rather than complete overhauls
- Test changes in limited areas before wider implementation
- Solicit feedback from all household members
- Document successful strategies for future reference

Advanced scheduling transforms smart lighting from a novelty into an essential home system that enhances daily life while reducing energy consumption. By thinking beyond simple timers to context-aware, adaptive systems, you'll achieve the full potential of your smart lighting investment.

Chapter 3: DIY Smart Thermostat Installation

What is a Smart Thermostat?

A smart thermostat represents a significant evolution from traditional temperature control devices. Unlike conventional programmable thermostats, smart thermostats connect to your home's Wi-Fi network, allowing remote access and control through smartphone applications. This connectivity enables a range of features that maximize both comfort and energy efficiency.

At its core, a smart thermostat performs the same fundamental function as any thermostat—it monitors your home's temperature and controls your heating, ventilation, and air conditioning (HVAC) system to maintain your desired temperature settings. However, smart thermostats integrate advanced technologies that transform this basic functionality into an intelligent home management system.

Key features that distinguish smart thermostats include:

Learning Capabilities: Many premium smart thermostats observe your temperature preferences over time and automatically create customized schedules based on your habits. For example, if you consistently lower the temperature before bedtime, the thermostat will begin making this adjustment automatically.

Occupancy Sensing: Using motion sensors, infrared detection, or geofencing through your smartphone's location, smart thermostats can determine when your home is occupied or empty, adjusting temperatures accordingly to avoid heating or cooling an empty house.

Energy Usage Reports: Smart thermostats track and analyze your energy consumption patterns, providing detailed reports that help you understand and optimize your usage. These insights often include comparisons to previous months and recommendations for potential savings.

Weather Responsiveness: By accessing weather forecasts through their internet connection, these devices can proactively adjust settings based on upcoming weather changes, ensuring optimal comfort while minimizing energy waste.

System Performance Monitoring: Many models can monitor your HVAC system's performance, alerting you to potential issues or maintenance needs before they become serious problems.

Integration with Smart Home Ecosystems: Smart thermostats typically work with popular smart home platforms like Amazon Alexa, Google Home, Apple HomeKit, and Samsung SmartThings, allowing for voice control and coordination with other smart devices in your home.

Beyond these technical capabilities, smart thermostats often feature intuitive touchscreen interfaces or color-changing displays that provide at-a-glance information about your home's current status and settings.

From an economic perspective, smart thermostats represent an investment that typically pays for itself through energy savings. The U.S. Environmental Protection Agency estimates that proper use of a programmable thermostat can save an average household about $180 per year in energy costs. Smart thermostats often exceed these savings by optimizing usage patterns more efficiently than standard programmable models.

Selecting a Thermostat: Best Models for DIYers

Choosing the right smart thermostat for your DIY installation requires balancing several factors, including compatibility with your existing HVAC system, desired features, budget constraints, and your personal technical comfort level. Here's a comprehensive guide to help you select the ideal model for your needs.

Compatibility Considerations

Before exploring specific models, determine your

HVAC system type:

C-Wire Requirement: Many smart thermostats require a C-wire (common wire) to provide continuous power. Check your existing thermostat wiring—if you don't have a C-wire, you'll either need a model that works without one, a power adapter kit, or to install a C-wire.

System Type Compatibility: Verify compatibility with your specific system:

- Conventional heating and cooling (most common)
- Heat pumps with auxiliary/emergency heat
- Multi-stage systems
- Radiator or in-floor heating systems
- Millivolt systems (like gas fireplaces)

Most manufacturers offer online compatibility checkers where you can input your current wiring configuration to confirm compatibility before purchasing.

Top DIY-Friendly Smart Thermostats

Ecobee SmartThermostat Premium

- *DIY-Friendly Features*: Includes a power extender kit for homes without C-wires; step-by-step installation app guidance; detailed wiring diagrams.
- *Technical Highlights*: Built-in air quality monitoring; dual-band Wi-Fi connectivity;

integrated Alexa voice assistant; comprehensive vacation settings.
- Installation Difficulty: Moderate
- *Price Range*: $230-$250

Google Nest Learning Thermostat (4th Generation)

- *DIY-Friendly Features*: Auto-detection of wiring during setup; built-in battery backup; can utilize heat-link technology instead of C-wire in some setups.
- *Technical Highlights*: True learning capabilities; elegant interface; Farsight technology detects your presence across the room.
- Installation Difficulty: Easy to Moderate
- *Price Range*: $240-$260

Honeywell Home T9 Smart Thermostat

- *DIY-Friendly Features*: Color-coded terminal labels; C-wire adapter included; exceptionally clear installation instructions.
- *Technical Highlights*: Room sensors with both temperature and humidity detection; 200-foot range for sensors; geofencing capability.
- Installation Difficulty: Easy
- *Price Range*: $170-$200

Amazon Smart Thermostat

- *DIY-Friendly Features*: Simplified design; fewer wiring options but extremely straightforward

setup; works with C-wire adapter (sold separately).
- *Technical Highlights*: Alexa integration; usage reports through the Alexa app; energy star certified.
- Installation Difficulty: Very Easy
- Price Range: $80-$100

Wyze Thermostat

- *DIY-Friendly Features*: Comprehensive compatibility check via app; includes adapter for non-C-wire setups; color-coded wiring terminals.
- *Technical Highlights*: Budget-friendly; learning schedule creation; maintenance reminders.
- Installation Difficulty: Moderate
- Price Range: $70-$90

Budget-Friendly Options

If you're cost-conscious but still want smart functionality, consider:

Emerson Sensi Wi-Fi Smart Thermostat

- Simple installation requiring minimal technical knowledge
- Works with most 24V HVAC systems
- C-wire optional for some systems
- Basic but reliable smart features
- Price Range: $90-$130

Honeywell Home T5+ Smart Thermostat

- Straightforward DIY installation
- Geofencing capability
- 7-day flexible scheduling
- Price Range: $120-$150

Feature Prioritization for DIYers

When evaluating features, DIY installers should prioritize:

1. **Installation Support**: Look for models offering detailed installation videos, responsive customer support, and troubleshooting guides.
2. **Wiring Flexibility**: Models that can adapt to various wiring configurations provide installation insurance.
3. **Setup Assistance**: App-based setup wizards can significantly simplify the configuration process.
4. **System Protection**: Advanced models include features that prevent damage to your HVAC equipment during improper installation attempts.
5. **Intuitive Interface**: A user-friendly interface reduces the learning curve after installation.

Remember that the most feature-rich thermostat isn't necessarily the best choice if it comes with a complicated installation process beyond your comfort level. For many DIYers, a balance between functionality and installation simplicity yields the most satisfying results.

Step-by-Step Installation: Wiring the Device to the

HVAC System

Installing a smart thermostat is a manageable DIY project that typically takes 30-60 minutes. Follow these comprehensive steps to ensure a successful installation:

Preparation Phase

1. Check Compatibility

- Confirm your HVAC system is compatible with your chosen smart thermostat
- Verify voltage requirements (most residential systems are 24V)
- Identify if you have a C-wire or need an adapter

2. Gather Necessary Tools

- Screwdriver (typically Phillips head)
- Wire stripper/cutter
- Drill and drill bits (if mounting requires new holes)
- Pencil
- Level
- Smartphone with thermostat manufacturer's app installed

3. Safety First

- Turn off power to your HVAC system at the circuit breaker

- Test by trying to turn on your current thermostat to confirm power is off
- Take a clear, well-lit photo of your existing thermostat's wiring before disconnecting anything

Removal of Old Thermostat

4. Remove Cover and Faceplate

- Carefully detach the cover of your existing thermostat
- Note the terminal labels where each wire connects (common labels include R, Rc, Rh, W, Y, G, C, O/B)

5. Label Wires

- Use the stickers typically included with your new thermostat to label each wire according to its terminal connection
- If no stickers are available, use masking tape and a pen
- Document the wire colors and their corresponding terminals in a note on your phone as backup

6. Disconnect Wires and Remove Mounting Plate

- Loosen terminal screws and carefully remove each wire
- Prevent wires from falling back into the wall by temporarily wrapping them around a pencil

- Unscrew the mounting plate from the wall

Installation of New Smart Thermostat

7. Install New Mounting Plate

- Position the new mounting plate level on the wall
- Mark screw positions if different from previous mounting holes
- If needed, drill pilot holes with appropriate bit size
- Feed wires through the central opening
- Secure the mounting plate with provided screws

8. Connect Wires to Appropriate Terminals

- Match each labeled wire to the corresponding terminal on the new thermostat base
- Insert bare wire ends fully into each terminal
- Tighten terminal screws securely without over-tightening
- Common wire connections include:
  - R, Rc, or Rh: Power (red)
  - G: Fan (green)
  - Y: Cooling (yellow)
  - W: Heating (white)
  - C: Common wire (various colors, often blue or black)
  - O/B: Reversing valve for heat pumps

9. Special Wiring Considerations

- **C-Wire Installation**: If your system lacks a C-wire:
  - ○ Option 1: Use the power adapter kit if included with your thermostat
  - ○ Option 2: Install a third-party C-wire adapter
  - ○ Option 3: Run a new C-wire from your HVAC control board (advanced)
- **Jumper Wire Setup**: Some systems require jumper connections between terminals (e.g., Rc to Rh) if your system uses a single transformer for both heating and cooling

10. Attach Display Unit/Faceplate

- Carefully align the display unit with the base
- Snap or screw the components together according to manufacturer instructions
- Ensure connection is secure

System Activation and Setup

11. Restore Power

- Return to your circuit breaker and restore power to the HVAC system
- Watch for the thermostat to power up or display startup indicators

12. Initial Configuration

- Follow the on-screen setup wizard or app-based instructions

- Connect to your home Wi-Fi network
- Register your device with the manufacturer
- Complete any firmware updates that may be required

13. System Testing

- Test heating function: Set temperature 5° above current room temperature
- Test cooling function: Set temperature 5° below current room temperature
- Test fan operation: Set fan to "On" rather than "Auto"
- Allow each system to run for 3-5 minutes to ensure proper function

14. Advanced Setup

- Configure temperature thresholds and differentials
- Set filter change reminders
- Enable any sensors included with your system
- Connect to your preferred smart home platform

Installation Verification

15. Final Checks

- Verify the thermostat maintains consistent power
- Confirm proper temperature readings
- Test remote access via smartphone app

- Ensure schedule programming functions correctly

By following these detailed steps, even those with minimal technical experience can successfully install a smart thermostat. If at any point you encounter unexpected wiring configurations or complications, don't hesitate to consult professional help rather than risking damage to your HVAC system.

Programming for Energy Savings: Set Schedules and Temperature Zones

Proper programming of your newly installed smart thermostat is crucial for maximizing energy efficiency and comfort. This section guides you through optimizing your settings to achieve significant energy savings while maintaining ideal home comfort.

Understanding Energy-Efficient Temperature Settings

Research from the U.S. Department of Energy suggests the following optimal temperature settings for energy efficiency:

- Heating Season:
  o When home and awake: 68°F (20°C)
  o When sleeping or away: 60-65°F (15-18°C)
- Cooling Season:
  o When home and awake: 78°F (26°C)
  o When sleeping or away: 82-85°F (28-29°C)

These recommendations can save approximately 10% annually on heating and cooling costs. However, your smart thermostat allows for personalized comfort while still achieving significant savings.

Creating Effective Schedules

Basic Schedule Creation

Most smart thermostats offer scheduling through their companion apps. To create an energy-efficient schedule:

1. **Identify Your Routine**: Map your typical weekday and weekend patterns, noting:
   o Wake-up times
   o Departure times
   o Return times
   o Bedtimes
2. **Program Temperature Changes**: Schedule temperature adjustments to occur:
   o 30 minutes before waking (for comfort upon rising)
   o 30-60 minutes before leaving (to maximize pre-departure efficiency)
   o 30 minutes before returning (for comfort upon arrival)
   o 30 minutes before bedtime (for optimal sleeping temperatures)
3. **Set Appropriate Differentials**: The temperature difference between your "home" and "away" settings should be substantial enough to

generate savings but not so extreme that your system works excessively to recover.

- o Recommended differential: 7-10°F for extended absences (8+ hours)
- o Recommended differential: 3-5°F for shorter absences (2-8 hours)

Advanced Scheduling Techniques

Beyond basic scheduling, explore these advanced programming options:

1. **Seasonal Schedule Adjustments**: Create separate heating and cooling season schedules that account for seasonal behavioral changes.
2. **Activity-Based Temperature Zones**: Program temperature adjustments based on typical activities:
   - o Cooking hours (kitchen heat generation may allow lower heating settings)
   - o Exercise periods (lower cooling temperatures during workout times)
   - o Guest entertaining (balance comfort and efficiency when hosting)
3. Vacation Mode Programming: For extended absences:
   - o Winter settings: 50-55°F (10-13°C) to prevent pipe freezing
   - o Summer settings: 85-90°F (29-32°C) to prevent humidity damage
   - o Schedule return to comfort temperatures 2-3 hours before your arrival

Leveraging Smart Learning Features

Many premium smart thermostats include learning capabilities that adapt to your preferences and behaviors:

Occupancy Detection Optimization:

- Position room sensors in frequently used areas
- Avoid placing sensors near drafts, direct sunlight, or heat sources
- For multi-sensor systems, prioritize readings from occupied rooms

Geofencing Configuration:

- Set appropriate radius boundaries (typically 1-3 miles from home)
- Enable geofencing for all household members' devices
- Configure appropriate "Home" and "Away" temperature settings
- Set minimum absence duration before triggering Away mode

Learning Algorithm Training:

- During the first 1-2 weeks, manually adjust temperatures to your preference
- Allow the system to observe these manual adjustments
- Provide feedback through the app when prompted about comfort levels

- Review and refine automated schedules after the learning period

Creating Temperature Zones Without Zoned HVAC

Even without a physically zoned HVAC system, smart thermostats with remote sensors can create virtual temperature zones:

1. Strategic Sensor Placement:
   - Bedrooms: Place sensors at bedside height for accurate sleeping condition readings
   - Living areas: Position sensors in frequently occupied seating areas
   - Problem areas: Add sensors to rooms that traditionally run too hot or cold
2. Zone Prioritization:
   - Day zones: During daytime hours, prioritize readings from living areas, home offices
   - Night zones: During sleeping hours, prioritize bedroom sensor readings
   - Custom zones: Create activity-based zones for weekend versus weekday usage
3. Sensor Averaging Configuration:
   - Determine whether your system should average all sensor readings
   - Configure which sensors should be included at different times
   - Test different combinations to find optimal comfort and efficiency

Integration with Other Smart Home Systems

Maximize efficiency by connecting your thermostat with other smart home elements:

1. **Smart Ceiling Fan Coordination**: Program fans to operate at higher speeds during thermostat setbacks to maintain comfort with less HVAC usage.
2. **Smart Blind/Shade Integration**: Automatically close blinds during peak summer heat and open them for solar gain in winter.
3. **Smart Vent Compatibility**: For advanced users, compatible smart vents can further enhance room-by-room temperature control.
4. **Smart Home Routines**: Create integrated routines such as:
   - "Goodnight" routine that adjusts temperature, closes blinds, and turns off lights
   - "Vacation" mode that coordinates thermostat setbacks with security lighting
   - "Home" routine that prepares your environment before you arrive

By thoroughly programming your smart thermostat and integrating it with your overall home ecosystem, you can achieve the perfect balance between comfort and energy efficiency. Most users report 10-25% energy savings after proper smart thermostat optimization, with the system typically paying for itself within 1-2 years of installation.

Common Installation Mistakes to Avoid

Even experienced DIYers can encounter challenges when installing smart thermostats. Being aware of these common pitfalls will help ensure your installation goes smoothly and your system operates efficiently.

Electrical Connection Errors

1. Improper Wire Identification

- **Mistake**: Assuming wire colors follow a universal standard.
- **Reality**: Wire colors vary widely between installations.
- **Solution**: Always identify wires by their terminal connections on the old thermostat, not by color. If terminal labels are worn or unclear, take a photo before disconnecting and consult HVAC documentation.

2. C-Wire Complications

- **Mistake**: Installing a smart thermostat without addressing C-wire requirements.
- **Reality**: Power-stealing thermostats or installations without proper common wire connections often lead to erratic behavior, system short-cycling, or complete failure.
- **Solution**: If your system lacks a C-wire:
  - Install the manufacturer's power adapter kit
  - Run a new C-wire from your HVAC control board

o Choose a smart thermostat specifically designed to work without a C-wire

3. Loose Wire Connections

- **Mistake**: Failing to secure wires properly in terminals.
- **Reality**: Loose connections cause intermittent operation or complete system failure.
- **Solution**: Ensure bare wire ends are straight, clean, and fully inserted into terminals. Tighten terminal screws securely but avoid over-tightening that might damage the wire.

4. Short Circuits from Exposed Wires

- **Mistake**: Leaving excessive bare wire exposed beyond terminal connections.
- **Reality**: Exposed wire can contact other terminals or metal components, causing shorts.
- **Solution**: Trim excess exposed wire, leaving only enough to make secure connections. If wires are frayed or damaged, cut back to fresh wire and strip approximately 1/4 inch of insulation.

Physical Installation Problems

5. Poor Thermostat Placement

- **Mistake**: Installing the thermostat in locations with temperature extremes.
- **Reality**: Inaccurate readings occur when thermostats are placed:

- In direct sunlight
- Near heat-generating appliances
- In drafty areas
- On exterior walls
- **Solution**: Mount the thermostat on an interior wall, away from direct sunlight, air vents, doorways, windows, and appliances, at approximately 5 feet from the floor.

6. Inadequate Wall Preparation

- **Mistake**: Mounting the thermostat on an uneven surface or failing to seal wall openings.
- **Reality**: Gaps around the thermostat allow drafts that affect temperature readings and can short electrical components.
- **Solution**: Use the mounting plate as a template to ensure level installation. For larger wall openings, use electrical outlet sealers or non-flammable insulation to block drafts.

7. Damaging Drywall During Removal

- **Mistake**: Forcefully removing an old thermostat that may be painted over or strongly adhered to the wall.
- **Reality**: Wall damage often necessitates repairs before installing the new thermostat.
- **Solution**: Use a utility knife to carefully score around the existing thermostat base. For painted-over units, gently use a putty knife to separate from the wall.

System Configuration Errors

8. Incorrect HVAC System Type Selection

- **Mistake**: Selecting the wrong system type during thermostat setup.
- **Reality**: Conventional systems, heat pumps, multi-stage systems, and dual-fuel systems all require different configuration settings.
- **Solution**: Verify your system type before installation by checking your HVAC model information or consulting your system's manual. During setup, select the precise configuration that matches your equipment.

9. Reversing Valve Setting Errors (Heat Pump Systems)

- **Mistake**: Incorrect O/B terminal configuration for heat pump reversing valves.
- **Reality**: Reversing valve orientation varies between manufacturers—some energize in cooling mode (O), others in heating mode (B).
- **Solution**: Consult your heat pump documentation to determine if your reversing valve is O-type (energized in cooling) or B-type (energized in heating) and configure accordingly.

10. Improper Voltage Matching

- **Mistake**: Installing a low-voltage thermostat on line-voltage heating systems.

- **Reality**: Most smart thermostats are designed for 24V systems and will be damaged if connected to 120V or 240V systems.
- **Solution**: Confirm your system voltage before purchasing. For line-voltage systems (common in baseboard heating), select specialty high-voltage smart thermostats or install a low-voltage relay.

Network and Software Issues

11. Inadequate Wi-Fi Signal

- **Mistake**: Installing in a location with poor Wi-Fi coverage.
- **Reality**: Weak signals cause connection drops, failed updates, and inability to control remotely.
- **Solution**: Test Wi-Fi signal strength at the installation location before mounting. If necessary, install a Wi-Fi extender or mesh network node to improve coverage.

12. Router Compatibility Problems

- **Mistake**: Assuming all routers work seamlessly with smart thermostats.
- **Reality**: Some older routers or those with unusual security settings may cause connection issues.
- **Solution**: Check the manufacturer's compatibility information. If problems persist, try:
  - Placing the thermostat on the 2.4GHz network (not 5GHz)

- Temporarily disabling complex security features during initial setup
- Updating router firmware

13. Skipping Firmware Updates

- **Mistake**: Ignoring prompted firmware updates during or after installation.
- **Reality**: Outdated firmware can result in performance issues, security vulnerabilities, or incompatibility with smart home systems.
- **Solution**: Complete all firmware updates during initial setup and enable automatic updates in settings.

Post-Installation Verification

14. Inadequate System Testing

- **Mistake**: Failing to test all HVAC functions after installation.
- **Reality**: Some issues only become apparent during certain modes of operation.
- **Solution**: Systematically test heating, cooling, fan-only operation, and any auxiliary or emergency heat functions before considering the installation complete.

15. Neglecting to Update Safety Systems

- **Mistake**: Overlooking integration with smoke/CO detectors or emergency shutoff features.

- **Reality**: Many smart thermostats can integrate with safety systems to shut down HVAC during emergencies, preventing circulation of smoke or carbon monoxide.
- **Solution**: Configure safety integrations if available, or consider adding compatible smart smoke/CO detectors to your system.

By avoiding these common installation mistakes, you significantly increase the likelihood of a successful smart thermostat installation and optimal system performance. When in doubt, consult manufacturer documentation or contact customer support rather than risking damage to your expensive HVAC equipment.

Troubleshooting: What to Do if Your Thermostat Isn't Working Correctly

Even with careful installation, you may encounter issues with your smart thermostat. This comprehensive troubleshooting guide will help you diagnose and resolve common problems without calling a professional.

Power and Display Issues

Problem: Thermostat Display is Blank or Unresponsive

Possible Causes:

1. Power interruption
2. C-wire connection issues

3. Circuit breaker tripped
4. Internal battery depleted (if applicable)

Troubleshooting Steps:

1. Check your electrical panel for tripped breakers related to HVAC system
2. Verify proper connection of R and C wires at both thermostat and furnace ends
3. If your model has a backup battery, replace it
4. Remove the thermostat from its base plate and reinstall, ensuring proper connection
5. Look for an internal reset button (usually a small pinhole) and press it using a paperclip

Problem: Thermostat Display Works But Shows Incorrect Information

Possible Causes:

1. Software glitch
2. Sensor calibration error
3. Poor placement affecting temperature readings

Troubleshooting Steps:

1. Perform a soft reset through the settings menu
2. Check for and install any available firmware updates
3. Verify the thermostat is not in direct sunlight or near heat sources
4. Use the calibration feature in advanced settings to adjust temperature readings

5. If using remote sensors, ensure they're properly paired and positioned

Connectivity and Network Issues

Problem: Thermostat Won't Connect to Wi-Fi

Possible Causes:

1. Weak Wi-Fi signal
2. Incorrect Wi-Fi password
3. Router compatibility issues
4. 2.4GHz vs. 5GHz network confusion

Troubleshooting Steps:

1. Verify Wi-Fi signal strength at thermostat location
2. Double-check Wi-Fi password for errors
3. Restart your router
4. Ensure you're connecting to a 2.4GHz network (most smart thermostats don't support 5GHz)
5. Temporarily disable any complex security settings during setup
6. Move your router closer or add a Wi-Fi extender

Problem: Thermostat Keeps Disconnecting from Network

Possible Causes:

1. Intermittent Wi-Fi signal
2. Router firmware issues

3. Thermostat firmware needs updating
4. Interference from other devices

Troubleshooting Steps:

1. Update router firmware
2. Change Wi-Fi channel on your router to reduce interference
3. Update thermostat firmware
4. Check if other Wi-Fi devices are experiencing similar issues
5. Add the thermostat's MAC address to your router's priority device list

HVAC System Control Problems

Problem: Heating or Cooling System Won't Turn On

Possible Causes:

1. Incorrect wiring connections
2. System switch set to wrong mode
3. Temperature setting not calling for heating/cooling
4. Safety lockout activated
5. Delay protection feature active

Troubleshooting Steps:

1. Verify system mode is set correctly (Heat, Cool, or Auto)

2. Set temperature at least 5 degrees above (for heating) or below (for cooling) current room temperature
3. Check for error codes on the thermostat display
4. Confirm that all wires are securely connected to correct terminals
5. Turn off power at the breaker for 1 minute, then restore power
6. Check furnace/AC unit for local power switches that may be off
7. Inspect for blown fuses on the HVAC control board

Problem: System Short Cycling (Turning On and Off Frequently)

Possible Causes:

1. Improper placement causing temperature fluctuations
2. Temperature differential set too narrow
3. Power-stealing thermostat without C-wire
4. Oversized HVAC system for the space

Troubleshooting Steps:

1. Adjust temperature differential settings (typically found in advanced/installer settings)
2. Install a C-wire or adapter if your thermostat is "power stealing"
3. Relocate thermostat away from drafts, sunlight, or heat sources
4. Check for blocked air returns or dirty air filters

5. Inspect ductwork for leaks or disconnections

Problem: Fan Operates Incorrectly

Possible Causes:

1. Improper G-wire connection
2. Fan settings configured incorrectly
3. Thermostat confusion between auto and on modes

Troubleshooting Steps:

1. Verify G-wire is securely connected at both thermostat and HVAC control board
2. Check fan settings in the thermostat menu (Auto, On, Circulate)
3. Test fan independently using the fan-only mode
4. Ensure the blower motor is functioning properly
5. Check for obstructions in ductwork

Smart Features and Scheduling Issues

Problem: Automatic Schedule Not Working Properly

Possible Causes:

1. Learning period not completed
2. Conflicting manual adjustments
3. Software glitch
4. Incorrect time/date settings

Troubleshooting Steps:

1. Verify the thermostat has the correct date, time, and time zone
2. Allow learning thermostats to complete their learning period (typically 1-2 weeks)
3. Review and clear any manual temperature overrides
4. Delete and recreate problematic schedules
5. Perform a factory reset if problems persist (note: this will erase all settings)

Problem: Geofencing or Home/Away Features Not Working

Possible Causes:

1. Location services disabled on smartphone
2. App running in background restricted
3. Geofence radius set incorrectly
4. Multiple users not properly configured

Troubleshooting Steps:

1. Ensure location services are enabled for the thermostat app on all household smartphones
2. Check app permissions to allow background operation
3. Adjust geofence radius in settings (typically 1-3 miles works best)
4. Verify all household members have properly configured accounts and devices
5. Toggle airplane mode on and off to reset phone connections

Advanced Diagnostic Methods

Checking Voltage at Thermostat: If you have a multimeter, you can perform voltage tests to diagnose wiring issues:

1. Set multimeter to AC voltage (24V range)
2. With thermostat removed but wires accessible, test between:
   - R and C: Should read approximately 24VAC
   - R and W: Should read 24VAC when calling for heat
   - R and Y: Should read 24VAC when calling for cooling
   - R and G: Should read 24VAC when fan is called

System Diagnostic Modes: Many smart thermostats include diagnostic modes accessible through installer menus:

1. Access installer settings (typically by holding specific button combinations)
2. Look for system test or diagnostic options
3. Run individual tests for heat, cool, fan, and auxiliary functions
4. Note any error codes displayed during testing

Factory Reset Procedure: As a last resort, performing a factory reset can resolve persistent software issues:

1. Back up any custom schedules if possible

2. Follow manufacturer's specific reset procedure (usually in settings menu or via hardware button)
3. After reset, reconfigure system type and installer settings before basic user settings
4. Update to latest firmware immediately after reset

When to Call a Professional

While many issues can be resolved through DIY troubleshooting, contact an HVAC professional if:

- You detect electrical burning smells
- Circuit breakers repeatedly trip when the system activates
- Your HVAC system makes unusual noises during operation
- You experience complete system failure that doesn't respond to power cycling
- The thermostat displays error codes that aren't addressed in the manual
- You've performed all troubleshooting steps without resolution

Remember that smart thermostat manufacturers typically offer extensive technical support through phone, chat, or email. Contact their customer service before calling an HVAC technician, as many issues can be resolved with their specialized guidance.

By systematically working through these troubleshooting steps, you can resolve most common smart thermostat issues and enjoy the comfort and efficiency benefits these devices provide.

Chapter 4: Building Your Own Smart Security System

Overview of DIY Security Systems

In today's connected world, home security has evolved far beyond the traditional alarm system. With the proliferation of affordable smart devices, homeowners can now build comprehensive security systems tailored to their specific needs without breaking the bank. DIY smart security systems offer flexibility, customization, and often lower costs compared to professionally installed solutions.

The core components of a modern DIY security system typically include:

- **Smart cameras**: Providing visual monitoring of your property, both indoors and outdoors
- **Sensors**: Detecting motion, door/window openings, glass breaks, and environmental conditions
- **Smart alarms**: Alerting you to potential intrusions or emergencies
- **Smart locks**: Securing entry points with keyless access
- **Central hub**: Coordinating all components and connecting to your smartphone

The beauty of building your own system lies in the ability to start small and expand as needed. You might begin with a single camera covering your front door, then gradually add door sensors, motion detectors, and eventually a comprehensive network of devices protecting every vulnerable area of your home.

Benefits of DIY Security Systems

Building your own security system offers several advantages over traditional security services:

Cost savings: Eliminate monthly monitoring fees and expensive installation costs. Most DIY systems operate on a one-time purchase model, with optional paid subscriptions for enhanced features like cloud storage.

Customization: Select only the components you need, positioning them exactly where they'll be most effective for your specific living space.

Expandability: Start with basic protection and add components as your needs change or budget allows.

Portability: Take your system with you when you move, unlike hardwired professional installations that stay with the property.

Tech integration: Easily integrate with other smart home devices like voice assistants, smart lights, and automated routines.

Understanding System Architecture

Before diving into component selection, it's important to understand how a smart security system works as a cohesive unit:

1. **Sensors and cameras** monitor your environment and detect changes or anomalies
2. **These devices communicate** with a central hub or directly with your router
3. **The hub processes information** and executes predetermined actions
4. **Notifications and alerts** are sent to your smartphone
5. **You can remotely view and control** your system through a dedicated app

Most modern systems operate wirelessly, communicating via Wi-Fi, Bluetooth, Zigbee, Z-Wave, or proprietary protocols. This wireless architecture simplifies installation but means you'll need reliable internet connectivity and sometimes strategic placement to ensure all devices maintain strong connections.

Selecting Equipment

The foundation of an effective DIY security system lies in choosing the right equipment for your specific needs. Let's explore each component category in detail.

Smart Cameras

Security cameras serve as the eyes of your system,

providing visual verification of events and valuable evidence if needed. When selecting cameras, consider these factors:

Resolution: Higher resolution cameras (1080p or 2K) provide clearer images that can capture important details like faces or license plates. While 4K cameras offer exceptional detail, they require more bandwidth and storage.

Field of view: Wide-angle lenses (110° or greater) cover more area with fewer cameras. Pan-tilt-zoom (PTZ) cameras can be remotely adjusted to monitor different areas.

Indoor vs. outdoor: Outdoor cameras require weather resistance (look for IP65 or higher ratings) and often include additional features like spotlights or sirens.

Power source: Wired cameras provide reliable power but require more complex installation. Battery-powered cameras offer flexible placement but need periodic recharging. Solar options can extend battery life.

Storage options: Consider whether footage is stored locally (on SD cards or a dedicated NVR), in the cloud (usually requiring a subscription), or both for redundancy.

Smart features: Look for motion detection, person recognition, activity zones, and night vision. Premium cameras may offer additional AI features like package detection or facial recognition.

Recommended starter cameras:

- For indoor use: Wyze Cam v3 offers exceptional value with 1080p resolution, person detection, and local storage options.
- For outdoor use: Eufy SoloCam E40 provides battery-powered convenience with 2K resolution and no required subscription fees.

Motion Detectors

Dedicated motion sensors offer broader coverage than camera-based motion detection and use less power. They're ideal for monitoring large rooms or areas where cameras might be impractical.

Technologies: Most consumer motion detectors use passive infrared (PIR) sensors that detect body heat. More advanced models might combine PIR with microwave or ultrasonic detection for fewer false alarms.

Pet immunity: If you have pets, look for motion sensors with pet immunity features that ignore movement from animals under a certain weight (typically 40-80 pounds).

Sensitivity and range: Consider the detection range (typically 25-40 feet) and adjustable sensitivity settings to minimize false alarms.

Placement considerations: Mount motion sensors at the optimal height (usually 6-8 feet) in corners for maximum coverage. Avoid locations near heating vents, direct sunlight, or moving objects that could trigger false alarms.

Door and Window Sensors

These simple but effective sensors form the first line of defense, alerting you whenever a door or window is opened.

Design options: Most door/window sensors consist of two pieces—a magnetic sensor and a transmitter—that trigger when separated. Low-profile designs minimize visibility.

Installation method: Adhesive-mounted sensors are easiest to install but may eventually lose adhesion. Screw-mounted options provide more permanent installation.

Additional features: Some advanced sensors include tamper detection, temperature sensing, or even light sensors that can detect if someone is using a flashlight inside your home at night.

Quantity planning: At minimum, secure all ground-level doors and windows. For comprehensive protection, include upstairs windows accessible from trees, roofs, or fire escapes.

Glass Break Sensors

While door/window sensors detect openings, glass break sensors can alert you if someone attempts to enter by breaking a window or glass door without opening it.

Detection methods: Acoustic glass break sensors listen for the specific frequency of breaking glass. Shock sensors detect vibrations from impact.

Coverage area: A single acoustic sensor can typically monitor windows within a 15-25 foot radius, making them more economical for rooms with multiple windows.

False alarm prevention: Modern glass break sensors use advanced algorithms to distinguish breaking glass from similar sounds like jingling keys or dropping items.

Environmental Sensors

A comprehensive security system protects not just against intruders but also environmental hazards:

Water leak sensors: Place near washing machines, water heaters, dishwashers, and under sinks to detect leaks before they cause significant damage.

Smoke and CO detectors: Smart versions can send alerts to your phone even when you're away from home.

Temperature sensors: Monitor for freezing conditions

that could lead to burst pipes or dangerous heat that could affect pets or sensitive items.

Smart Alarms

Audible alarms serve both as deterrents and alerts:

Siren types: Indoor sirens are typically 95-105 dB, while outdoor sirens can reach 110+ dB. Some include strobe lights for visual alerts.

Power options: Battery-powered sirens continue functioning during power outages. Some include backup batteries for normally wired operation.

Trigger options: Configure sirens to activate based on specific events (motion detection, door openings) or manually via app.

Smart features: Some sirens double as chimes for doors or include pre-recorded voice messages that can announce which zone has been triggered.

Smart Locks

Smart locks provide keyless entry and remote access control:

Lock types: Smart locks come as complete replacements or retrofits that attach to existing deadbolts. Retrofit options are generally easier to install and allow you to keep your existing keys.

Access methods: Consider whether you want keypad

entry, fingerprint reading, app control, or a combination of these options.

Power considerations: Most smart locks run on batteries that last 3-12 months. Look for models that provide low battery warnings well in advance and have backup entry methods.

Integration capabilities: Ensure compatibility with your chosen security system and other smart home platforms like Amazon Alexa, Google Home, or Apple HomeKit.

Central Hub or Controller

The hub serves as the brain of your system, coordinating all components:

Standalone vs. integrated: Some systems require a dedicated hub, while others might use a smart speaker or your smartphone as the controller.

Protocol compatibility: Ensure your hub supports all the wireless protocols used by your devices (Wi-Fi, Z-Wave, Zigbee, etc.).

Backup options: Look for hubs with battery backup and cellular backup options to maintain protection during power or internet outages.

Local vs. cloud processing: Systems that can process data locally offer better privacy and continue functioning during internet outages.

Step-by-Step Project: Setting Up Cameras and Integration

Now that we've covered the components, let's walk through a practical implementation of a basic camera system integrated with a smart hub.

Planning Your Camera Setup

1. **Map your property**: Create a simple floor plan of your home and mark vulnerable areas:
   - Entry points: front door, back door, ground-floor windows
   - Valuable storage areas: home office, jewelry storage
   - Common entry paths: driveway, walkways, backyard access points
2. **Determine camera quantity and placement**:
   - Front door: A doorbell camera or focused entryway camera
   - Backyard: Wide-angle camera covering the entire space
   - Driveway/side access: Motion-activated camera with good night vision
   - Indoor common areas: Living room or hallway camera covering multiple rooms
3. **Check infrastructure requirements**:
   - Power outlets for wired cameras or charging locations for battery cameras
   - Wi-Fi coverage throughout camera locations (consider mesh Wi-Fi if needed)
   - Storage needs based on camera quantity

and recording preferences

Installation Process

Installing an Indoor Camera

1. **Unbox and prepare the camera:**
   - Remove all packaging
   - If applicable, insert microSD card for local storage
   - Plug in the power adapter
2. **Download the manufacturer's app:**
   - Create an account if you don't already have one
   - Follow the app's instructions for adding a new device
   - Most apps will guide you through connecting the camera to your Wi-Fi
3. **Physical installation:**
   - For tabletop placement: Simply position the camera with a clear view of the area
   - For wall mounting:
     - Use the included mounting template to mark screw holes
     - Drill pilot holes if mounting on drywall
     - Secure the mount with included screws
     - Attach the camera to the mount
     - Adjust angle for optimal coverage
4. **Configure settings:**
   - Set up motion detection zones to focus on

important areas
- o Adjust sensitivity to prevent false alarms
- o Configure notification preferences
- o Set recording schedules if desired

Installing an Outdoor Camera

1. **Preparation**:
   - o For battery-powered cameras: Fully charge the battery before installation
   - o For wired cameras: Ensure power source availability and plan cable routing
2. **App setup**:
   - o Similar to indoor cameras, download the app and create an account
   - o Follow guided setup for the specific model
3. **Physical installation**:
   - o Choose a location 7-10 feet above ground level
   - o Ensure the camera is within Wi-Fi range (test before permanent mounting)
   - o For wired cameras:
     - ▪ Turn off power at the circuit breaker if connecting to household electrical
     - ▪ Use weatherproof cable covers for exposed wiring
     - ▪ Consider hiring an electrician if you're uncomfortable working with electrical wiring
   - o For battery cameras:
     - ▪ Use included mounting bracket
     - ▪ Position away from direct sun

exposure if possible to extend
battery life
4. **Weather protection**:
    - o Ensure the camera is rated for outdoor use
      (IP65 or higher)
    - o Position under eaves or use weather
      shields where possible
    - o Seal any drill holes with silicone caulk to
      prevent water intrusion
5. **Configuration**:
    - o Set up activity zones to ignore public areas
      like sidewalks
    - o Adjust motion sensitivity based on
      distance to common pathways
    - o Enable night vision and test in low-light
      conditions

Integrating with a Smart Hub

Once your cameras are installed, integrating them
with a central hub provides unified control and
automation capabilities.

1. **Hub setup**:
    - o Position your hub centrally in your home
      for optimal connectivity
    - o Connect to power and your internet router
    - o Follow manufacturer instructions to set up
      the hub via its app
2. **Adding cameras to the hub**:
    - o Most modern hubs use discovery to find
      compatible devices

- Select "Add device" in your hub's app
- Choose the camera category
- Follow prompts to connect each camera
- For non-native integration, check if IFTTT, Alexa, or Google Home can bridge the connection

3. **Creating basic automations**:
   - Motion-triggered recording: Set cameras to record when motion is detected
   - Light coordination: Configure outdoor lights to activate when cameras detect motion
   - Notification rules: Customize which events trigger smartphone alerts
   - Scheduling: Set different modes for home, away, and night time

4. **Testing the system**:
   - Perform a walk test to ensure motion detection works as expected
   - Test night vision capabilities after dark
   - Verify that all notifications arrive promptly
   - Check that recordings are properly stored and accessible

DIY Alarm System: Building a Basic Alarm with a Smart Controller

While cameras provide monitoring, a proper alarm system adds active deterrence. Here's how to build a basic but effective alarm system centered around a smart controller.

Components Selection

1. **Smart hub with alarm functionality**:
   - Popular options include Samsung SmartThings, Ring Alarm, or Hubitat
   - Ensure the hub supports battery backup and, ideally, cellular backup
2. **Entry sensors** for all doors and ground-floor windows
3. **Motion sensors** for key areas:
   - Main hallway
   - Living room
   - Master bedroom
   - Basement entry
4. **Indoor siren** (95-105 dB) for alerting occupants
5. **Outdoor siren** (optional but recommended) to alert neighbors and deter intruders
6. **Panic buttons** strategically placed:
   - Master bedroom
   - Kitchen
   - Home office

Installation Walkthrough

1. **Hub placement and setup**:
   - Position centrally for optimal wireless coverage
   - Connect to your router via ethernet for most reliable performance
   - Install backup batteries if applicable
   - Set up cellular backup (if available) for protection during internet outages

2. **Door/window sensor installation**:
   - Clean mounting surfaces with alcohol
   - Align sensors so magnetic components meet when closed
   - Apply strong adhesive or use screws for permanent installation
   - Test each sensor after installation
   - Label each sensor in your app with specific location (e.g., "Kitchen Window")
3. **Motion detector placement**:
   - Mount in corners at 7-8 feet height
   - Avoid areas with heating vents or direct sunlight
   - Position to cover entry paths rather than areas with frequent movement
   - Test detection range and adjust sensitivity as needed
4. **Siren installation**:
   - Indoor: Mount on ceiling or high wall in central location
   - Outdoor: Position under eaves for weather protection
   - Connect to power source or install batteries
   - Test at reduced volume if possible to avoid disturbing neighbors
5. **Panic button setup**:
   - Mount at accessible height in discreet locations
   - Program for silent alarm or full siren response based on preference
   - Test functionality regularly

Configuration and Testing

1. **Zone setup**:
   - Create logical groupings (perimeter, interior, sleeping areas)
   - Configure appropriate responses for each zone
2. **Mode configuration**:
   - Home mode: Interior motion sensors disabled, perimeter protection active
   - Away mode: Full system activation
   - Night mode: Perimeter plus downstairs motion sensors active
   - Vacation mode: Additional sensitivity and recording options
3. **Response rules**:
   - Immediate notifications for all triggers
   - Siren activation after entry sensor trigger with 30-60 second delay
   - Instant siren for glass break or interior motion when armed
   - Sequential triggers (multiple sensors) escalate response
4. **System testing**:
   - Test each component individually
   - Perform full system tests in each mode
   - Verify notification delivery to all authorized users
   - Practice disarming procedures with all family members

Smart Lock Setup: DIY Installation of Smart Locks

Smart locks represent one of the most immediately useful security upgrades, eliminating keys and enabling remote access control.

Selecting the Right Smart Lock

1. **Replacement vs. retrofit:**
   - Full replacements substitute your entire lock mechanism
   - Retrofits attach to your existing deadbolt for easier installation
2. **Access methods:**
   - Keypad: Convenient for family and temporary access codes
   - Fingerprint: Fast and secure but typically more expensive
   - App-based: Requires smartphone access
   - Key backup: Essential for power outages
3. **Compatibility considerations:**
   - Door thickness and preparation (standard vs. custom)
   - Existing deadbolt compatibility for retrofit options
   - Smart home platform integration (Alexa, Google, HomeKit)
   - Connection type (Bluetooth, Wi-Fi, Z-Wave, Zigbee)

Installation Process

For Retrofit Smart Locks

1. **Preparation:**

- Check compatibility with your existing deadbolt
- Install fresh batteries in the smart lock
- Download manufacturer's app

2. **Installation steps:**
   - Remove the interior thumb turn plate from your existing deadbolt
   - Attach the mounting plate to the door using existing screws
   - Connect the tailpiece adapter to your deadbolt's tailpiece
   - Attach the smart lock to the mounting plate
   - Secure with included screws
   - Install batteries

3. **Configuration:**
   - Follow app instructions to connect to your smartphone
   - Calibrate the lock following manufacturer guidelines
   - Test manual operation
   - Create access codes for family members

For Full Replacement Smart Locks

1. **Removing existing lock:**
   - Unscrew interior hardware
   - Remove deadbolt mechanism
   - Extract exterior keyhole assembly

2. **Preparing the door:**
   - Clean the edge bore and cross bore holes
   - Adjust latch plate if needed

- Ensure strike plate alignment
3. **Installing new smart lock:**
   - Insert latch assembly into edge bore
   - Feed connection cables through cross bore
   - Mount exterior keypad/lock body
   - Connect cables to interior assembly
   - Attach interior assembly with mounting screws
   - Install batteries
4. **Configuration:**
   - Connect to smartphone via manufacturer's app
   - Program master code
   - Set up additional access codes
   - Configure auto-lock features
   - Test operation multiple times

Integration with Security System

1. **Connecting to your hub:**
   - Add lock to your smart home system following app instructions
   - Ensure proper communication between devices
2. **Creating automations:**
   - Auto-lock after set period of being unlocked
   - Security system arming when door locks
   - Disarming system when unlocked with specific codes
   - Temporary access codes for service providers that expire automatically

3. **Security best practices**:
   - ○ Change default codes immediately
   - ○ Use unique codes for each person
   - ○ Regularly audit access logs
   - ○ Update firmware when available
   - ○ Consider using two-factor authentication for app access

Troubleshooting Tips

Even well-planned DIY security systems can encounter issues. Here are solutions to common problems:

Connectivity Issues

1. **Device offline or unresponsive**:
   - ○ Check battery levels or power connections
   - ○ Verify Wi-Fi signal strength at device location
   - ○ Restart the device
   - ○ Reset and reconnect if necessary
   - ○ Consider a Wi-Fi extender or mesh network for consistent coverage
2. **Hub communication failures**:
   - ○ Ensure hub is centrally located
   - ○ Check for interference from other devices
   - ○ Verify router is functioning properly
   - ○ Update hub firmware
   - ○ Consider Z-Wave or Zigbee repeaters for extended range

False Alarms

1. **Motion detector false positives**:
   - Adjust sensitivity settings
   - Reposition away from heat sources, moving objects, or direct sunlight
   - Switch to pet-immune sensors if pets are triggering alarms
   - Create specific activity zones that exclude problem areas
2. **Door/window sensor issues**:
   - Realign magnetic components
   - Check for loose mounting
   - Replace batteries
   - Adjust sensitivity for sensors with adjustable triggering distance

Camera Problems

1. **Poor image quality**:
   - Clean camera lens
   - Check internet upload speed (minimum 2 Mbps recommended)
   - Reduce resolution if bandwidth is limited
   - Adjust positioning to improve lighting
2. **Night vision issues**:
   - Remove any physical obstructions
   - Clean IR illuminators
   - Position away from reflective surfaces
   - Add supplemental IR illuminators for extended range

Smart Lock Malfunctions

1. **Lock jams or doesn't fully engage**:

- Check door alignment and adjust hinges if needed
- Lubricate mechanical components with graphite powder
- Calibrate the lock following manufacturer instructions
- Ensure deadbolt properly aligns with strike plate

2. **Battery drainage issues:**
   - Use high-quality alkaline or lithium batteries
   - Check for obstructions causing motor strain
   - Reduce polling frequency in settings if possible
   - Consider whether extreme temperatures are affecting battery life

System Performance Optimization

1. **Reducing notification fatigue:**
   - Adjust motion sensitivity
   - Create specific alert schedules
   - Use person detection to filter out non-human motion
   - Create zones for high-traffic areas

2. **Improving response time:**
   - Prioritize local processing over cloud when possible
   - Ensure adequate internet bandwidth
   - Position hub centrally
   - Use wired connections for critical

components

Ensuring Privacy and Security: Safeguarding Data

A security system shouldn't become a vulnerability itself. Protecting your system from hackers and ensuring your privacy is essential.

Network Security

1. **Secure your Wi-Fi network**:
   - Use WPA3 encryption when available
   - Create strong, unique passwords
   - Change default router credentials
   - Keep router firmware updated
   - Consider a separate IoT network for smart devices
2. **Firewall and router settings**:
   - Enable firewall protection
   - Disable remote management
   - Turn off Universal Plug and Play (UPnP) if not needed
   - Use DNS security services for added protection

Device Security

1. **Update firmware regularly**:
   - Enable automatic updates when available
   - Check manufacturer websites for updates
   - Replace devices that no longer receive security updates
2. **Secure account credentials**:

- Use unique, strong passwords for each service
- Enable two-factor authentication
- Avoid sharing accounts among multiple users
- Create separate user accounts with appropriate permissions

3. **Secure physical access**:
    - Protect hub devices from tampering
    - Secure network equipment
    - Consider tamper-evident seals on critical components

Privacy Considerations

1. **Camera placement ethics**:
    - Avoid positioning cameras where they could view neighbors' property
    - Place indoor cameras with respect for private areas
    - Disable indoor cameras when privacy is desired using schedules or manual controls
    - Consider privacy shutters for indoor cameras
2. **Data storage policies**:
    - Understand how your data is used by service providers
    - Read privacy policies before committing to services
    - Consider local storage options to maintain control of footage
    - Set appropriate retention periods for

recordings
3. **Access controls**:
    - Limit guest access to view-only when possible
    - Regularly audit who has access to your system
    - Revoke access immediately when no longer needed
    - Use temporary codes for service providers

Legal Considerations

1. **Recording consent**:
    - Understand local laws regarding video and audio recording
    - Post notices about camera recording where legally required
    - Disable audio recording in jurisdictions requiring two-party consent
    - Be particularly careful with cameras that might capture public areas
2. **Footage usage limitations**:
    - Understand how footage can be legally used
    - Follow proper procedures when providing footage to authorities
    - Securely store evidence of security incidents
    - Consider consulting legal counsel for complex situations

The Future of DIY Security

Building your own smart security system offers unparalleled customization, control, and cost savings. As technology continues to advance, DIY systems will become even more powerful and user-friendly.

Emerging trends to watch include:

- **AI-powered analytics**: Increasingly sophisticated algorithms that can distinguish between humans, animals, vehicles, and packages
- **Cross-platform integration**: Better cooperation between different manufacturers and protocols
- **Voice control enhancements**: More natural and secure voice commands for security functions
- **Advanced environmental monitoring**: Detection of air quality, dangerous gas levels, and other hazards
- **Biometric advancements**: More affordable and reliable fingerprint, facial recognition, and other biometric security features

By building your system now, you create a flexible foundation that can evolve with these advancements. Start with the basics outlined in this chapter, then expand and upgrade as your needs change and technology improves.

Remember that the most effective security system is one that fits your specific needs, is properly maintained, and becomes a natural part of your daily routine. With the approach outlined in this chapter, you'll have not just greater security, but also greater peace of mind knowing you've built a system that perfectly suits your home and lifestyle.

Chapter 5: Voice Control Setup and Automation

Overview of Voice Assistants

Voice assistants have revolutionized how we interact with our smart homes, offering hands-free control and integration capabilities that bring convenience to daily living. Understanding the strengths, limitations, and unique features of each major platform will help you select the right voice assistant for your needs.

Amazon Alexa

Amazon's voice assistant has grown from a simple speaker to an extensive ecosystem that powers millions of smart homes worldwide.

Core Capabilities

- **Device Support**: Alexa boasts compatibility with over 100,000 smart home devices from more than 9,500 brands, making it the most widely supported voice assistant platform.

- **Wake Word Options**: While "Alexa" is the default wake word, you can change it to "Echo," "Amazon," or "Computer" to better suit your preferences.

- **Voice Recognition**: Alexa can recognize different household members' voices to provide personalized responses and access to individual calendars, shopping lists, and music preferences.

- **Routines**: Create multi-step automations triggered by voice commands, schedules, device status, or location.

- **Skills**: Expandable functionality through third-party "skills" (over 100,000 available) that add new capabilities from games to meditation guides.

Hardware Options

- **Echo Devices**: Amazon offers a range of Echo smart speakers and displays at various price points:
    - Echo Dot: Compact, affordable entry point
    - Echo: Standard speaker with improved audio
    - Echo Studio: Premium speaker with spatial audio
    - Echo Show: Smart displays with screens ranging from 5" to 15"
    - Echo Flex: Plug-in mini speaker for spaces where a full speaker isn't needed

- **Third-Party Integration**: Many third-party speakers, appliances, and even cars now incorporate Alexa functionality.

Strengths

- **Smart Home Integration**: Unmatched device compatibility across brands and categories

- **Buying Options**: Wide range of first-party devices at various price points

- **Skill Ecosystem**: Extensive library of third-party extensions

- **Shopping Integration**: Seamless Amazon shopping experience for Prime members

- **Whole-Home Audio**: Easy multi-room music playback

Limitations

- **Natural Conversation**: Sometimes requires specific phrasing compared to other assistants

- **Knowledge Queries**: Less adept at answering complex questions compared to Google Assistant

- **Privacy Concerns**: Past controversies regarding recording reviews by human employees

Google Assistant

Google's AI-powered assistant leverages the company's search expertise to deliver a conversational experience that excels at answering questions and integrating with Google services.

Core Capabilities

- **Natural Language Processing**: Google Assistant understands context and conversational cues better than most competitors, allowing for more natural interactions.

- **Knowledge Graph**: Access to Google's vast knowledge graph makes it exceptional at answering factual questions and providing useful information.

- **Voice Match**: Can recognize up to six different voices per household for personalized responses.

- **Routines**: Create custom sequences of actions triggered by specific phrases, times, or events.

- **Continued Conversation**: Ability to ask follow-up questions without repeating the wake phrase.

Hardware Options

- **Nest Smart Speakers and Displays**:

  - Nest Mini: Compact, affordable smart speaker

  - Nest Audio: Mid-range speaker with improved sound quality

  - Nest Hub: Smart display with 7" screen

  - Nest Hub Max: Larger 10" display with built-in camera

- **Third-Party Devices**: Many Android phones, watches, TVs, and other manufacturers' products incorporate Google Assistant.

Strengths

- **Conversational Ability**: More natural dialogue flow with better contextual understanding

- **Search Capabilities**: Superior at answering factual questions and web searches

- **Google Services Integration**: Seamless connection with Gmail, Calendar, Maps, and other Google services

- **Broadcast Feature**: Use as a whole-home intercom system

- **Translation**: Real-time translation capabilities across numerous languages

Limitations

- **Smart Home Compatibility**: While extensive, has fewer compatible devices than Alexa

- **Shopping Experience**: Less integrated shopping functionality

- **Hardware Options**: Fewer first-party device options compared to Amazon

Comparing Voice Assistants for Your Smart Home

When selecting a voice assistant platform, consider these factors:

Ecosystem Compatibility

- **Existing Devices**: If you already own smart home products, check which assistant they work with best.

- **Preferred Services**: Choose the assistant that integrates with the music, calendar, email, and shopping services you use most frequently.

- **Mobile Platform**: Google Assistant typically works more seamlessly with Android, while Alexa works equally well with both iOS and Android.

Daily Usage Patterns

- **Information Queries**: If you frequently ask factual questions, Google Assistant may be preferable.

- **Smart Home Control**: For extensive device control across many brands, Alexa offers the broadest compatibility.

- **Shopping**: Frequent Amazon shoppers will benefit from Alexa's integration with Amazon services.

Multi-Assistant Strategies

Many smart homes actually benefit from utilizing multiple voice assistant platforms:

- **Zone-Based Deployment**: Use Google Assistant in areas where information queries are common (office, kitchen) and Alexa in areas focused on smart home control or entertainment.

- **Task Specialization**: Leverage each assistant's strengths for different functions (Google for calendar management, Alexa for shopping and smart home control).

- **Redundancy**: Having multiple systems provides backup options if one service experiences an outage.

Setting Up Voice Control for Smart Devices

Implementing voice control requires thoughtful planning and setup to ensure reliable, intuitive operation throughout your home. This section guides you through the process of creating a voice-controlled environment that responds naturally to your commands.

Strategic Device Placement

The effectiveness of voice control begins with proper placement of voice assistant devices:

Coverage Planning

- **Room Analysis**: Evaluate each room's size, acoustics, and typical activities to determine device needs.

- **Activity Zones**: Place devices in areas where voice control is most beneficial—near entryways, in kitchens where hands may be occupied, and in living areas where smart home control is frequent.

- **Distance Considerations**: Most voice assistants can hear normal speaking voices within approximately 20-25 feet in optimal conditions, though background noise may reduce this range.

- **Multi-Room Coverage**: For larger homes, plan overlapping coverage to ensure commands can be heard anywhere without shouting.

Acoustic Optimization

- **Avoid Interference**: Position devices away from noisy appliances, air vents, or speakers that might interfere with voice recognition.

- **Hard Surfaces**: Rooms with many hard surfaces create echoes that can degrade voice recognition; consider acoustic treatments in problematic spaces.

- **Height Placement**: For optimal pickup, position voice assistants at ear height when possible, or at least away from walls or objects that might block sound.

Initial Setup and Configuration

Getting started with your chosen voice assistant platform requires several key steps:

Device Setup Process

1. **Download the App**: Install the companion app (Alexa or Google Home) on your smartphone.

2. **Create or Login to Account**: Set up a new account or sign in with your existing Amazon or Google credentials.

3. **Add Device**: Follow in-app instructions to connect your smart speaker or display to your Wi-Fi network.

4. **Voice Training**: Complete voice recognition training if offered to improve recognition accuracy.

5. **Location Settings**: Set the correct address and time zone for local information and accurate automation timing.

Basic Voice Assistant Settings

- **Wake Word Sensitivity**: Adjust how easily the device activates upon hearing its wake word (particularly useful in noisy environments or for deaf or hard-of-hearing users).

- **Voice Purchasing**: Configure or disable voice purchasing capabilities to prevent unauthorized orders.

- **Do Not Disturb**: Set quiet hours when notifications and announcements are silenced.

- **Voice Recognition**: Train the assistant to recognize different household members for personalized responses.

- **Default Services**: Select preferred music, video, and shopping services for streamlined requests.

Connecting Smart Home Devices

Integrating your existing smart home devices with voice control expands functionality and convenience:

Device Discovery

1. **Enable Skills/Services**: Add the appropriate skill (Alexa) or service (Google) for your smart home devices through the assistant's app.

2. **Device Discovery**: Initiate device discovery through the app or with voice commands like "Alexa, discover devices" or "Hey Google, sync my devices."

3. **Manual Addition**: For devices not automatically discovered, add them manually through the app using manufacturer instructions.

Grouping and Naming

- **Room-Based Groups**: Create logical room groupings (e.g., "Living Room," "Kitchen") to control multiple devices with a single command.

- **Custom Groups**: Create functional groups that span multiple rooms (e.g., "Downstairs Lights," "Night Mode").

- **Intuitive Naming**: Use clear, distinctive names that are easy to pronounce and unlikely to be confused with other commands.

- **Naming Conventions**: Establish consistent naming patterns like "Room + Device Type + Descriptor" (e.g., "Kitchen Pendant Light" or "Master Bedroom Fan").

Voice Command Testing

- **Test Basic Commands**: Verify that fundamental commands work for each device and group.

- **Try Variations**: Test different phrasings to identify the most reliable command structures.

- **Document Success**: Keep track of commands that work consistently for future reference and training other household members.

Voice Control Best Practices

Maximize reliability and usability with these proven approaches:

Command Structure Optimization

- **Be Specific**: Include both the device name and action in commands ("Alexa, turn on the living room lamp" rather than "Alexa, turn on the lamp").

- **Use Established Phrases**: Stick to common verbs like "turn on/off," "dim," "brighten," "set," and "adjust" that assistants recognize reliably.

- **Group Commands**: For frequent multi-device operations, create groups instead of controlling devices individually.

- **Percentage Values**: Use percentage values for dimming ("Alexa, set kitchen lights to 50%") for more precise control.

User Training

- **Family Onboarding**: Teach household members the most effective commands and naming conventions.

- **Command Lists**: Create a simple reference document of common commands for guests and family members.

- **Verbal Feedback**: Pay attention to how the assistant responds to confirm it understood your intent correctly.

- **Progressive Learning**: Start with basic commands before attempting more complex multi-step routines.

Privacy Considerations

- **Mute Options**: Familiarize yourself with how to quickly mute microphones when privacy is desired.

- **History Management**: Regularly review and delete voice history through the assistant's app.

- **Guest Awareness**: Inform visitors that voice assistants are active in your home.

- **Recording Settings**: Adjust settings regarding recording storage and review according to your comfort level.

DIY Project: Create Voice-Controlled Routines

One of the most powerful aspects of voice assistants is their ability to execute multiple actions with a single command. By creating customized routines, you can orchestrate complex sequences that transform how you interact with your home.

Understanding Voice-Controlled Routines

Routines combine multiple actions that execute automatically when triggered by a specific phrase, time, or event:

Routine Capabilities

- **Multi-Device Control**: Adjust multiple devices simultaneously across different manufacturers and categories.

- **Sequential Actions**: Execute actions in a specific order with timed delays between steps.

- **Service Integration**: Incorporate weather reports, news briefings, calendar information, and more.

- **Custom Responses**: Personalize what your assistant says when confirming routine execution.

- **Scene Creation**: Set specific states across multiple devices to create ambiance or functional modes.

Trigger Types

- **Voice Commands**: Custom phrases that initiate the routine (e.g., "Alexa, movie time" or "Hey Google, good morning").

- **Scheduled Times**: Set routines to run automatically at specific times or days of the week.

- **Device Status**: Trigger routines when specific devices change state (e.g., when a door sensor opens).

- **Location**: Activate routines when you arrive at or leave home (requires smartphone location access).

- **Alarm Dismissal**: Execute routines when you dismiss an alarm on your smart device.

Project: Creating a Morning Routine

Let's walk through the process of creating a comprehensive morning routine using voice assistants:

Planning Your Routine

1. **Identify Goals**: Define what you want your morning routine to accomplish (e.g., gentle wake-up, information delivery, home preparation).

2. **List Actions**: Outline each specific action in your desired sequence:

   - Gradually increase bedroom lights

   - Adjust thermostat to comfortable morning temperature

   - Present weather forecast and calendar events

   - Start coffee maker

   - Play morning news or music

3. **Determine Timing**: Decide whether to use a specific wake-up time, alarm dismissal, or voice command as your trigger.

4. **Device Inventory**: Verify that all required devices are compatible and connected to your voice assistant.

Step-by-Step Implementation

For Amazon Alexa:

1. Open the Alexa app and select "Routines" from the menu.

2. Tap the "+" icon to create a new routine.

3. Select a trigger type:

   o For voice trigger: Enter a custom phrase like "Alexa, good morning"

   o For scheduled trigger: Select time, frequency, and which device announces it

4. Add actions in your desired sequence:

   o Smart Home: Select devices and their actions (e.g., lights to 30% brightness)

   o Wait: Add delays between actions (e.g., 1 minute between light adjustments)

   o Weather: Add a weather report for your location

   o Traffic: Include commute information if relevant

- News: Add your preferred news briefing

- Music: Select music service and content

5. Review and save your routine.

For Google Assistant:

1. Open the Google Home app and tap "Routines."

2. Select "Add a routine" or tap the "+" button.

3. Configure your starter:

   - Voice command: Enter phrases like "Hey Google, I'm awake"

   - Schedule: Set specific times and days

4. Add actions:

   - Adjust home devices: Control lights, thermostats, or other smart devices

   - Communicate and announce: Add weather, calendar, reminders, or news

   - Adjust media: Set volume and play music or radio

   - Add delays: Insert waits between actions

5. Review and save your routine.

Testing and Refinement

1. **Initial Test**: Trigger your routine and observe the execution.

2. **Timing Adjustments**: Modify delays between actions if the sequence feels rushed or too slow.

3. **Command Tweaking**: Refine voice triggers if you encounter activation issues.

4. **Progressive Enhancement**: Once your basic routine works reliably, add more sophisticated elements.

Project: Evening Wind-Down Routine

Create a routine to help transition your household toward bedtime:

Implementation Guide

1. **Set up the trigger**: Create a voice command like "Alexa, time to wind down" or "Hey Google, begin bedtime routine."

2. **Add actions in sequence**:
   - Dim living area lights to 30%
   - Turn on bedroom and bathroom lights at a warm color temperature (2700K or lower)
   - Adjust thermostat to optimal sleeping temperature (typically 65-68°F/18-20°C)
   - Turn off TVs and entertainment systems
   - Play relaxing music at low volume
   - After 30 minutes, dim bedroom lights further
   - After 60 minutes, turn off all lights except night lights

3. **Add personalized elements**:

- Weather forecast for tomorrow

- Gentle reminder of tomorrow's first appointment

- Confirmation that doors are locked and security system is armed

Advanced Customizations

- **Person-Specific Variations**: Create different versions for different household members.

- **Weekday vs. Weekend**: Adjust timing and actions based on different schedules.

- **Seasonal Adjustments**: Incorporate different lighting or temperature settings based on time of year.

- **Sleep Tracking Integration**: If you use sleep tracking devices, incorporate them into your routine.

Project: Custom Voice Command for Entertainment

Create a seamless entertainment experience activated by voice:

Implementation Steps

1. **Define your command**: "Alexa, movie night" or "Hey Google, it's showtime."

2. **Configure entertainment-specific actions**:

   - Dim or turn off lights in viewing area

- o Turn on accent or bias lighting behind the TV

- o Power on TV and sound system to appropriate inputs

- o Set thermostat to comfortable viewing temperature

- o Close motorized blinds or shades if available

3. **Add convenient extras:**

   - o Notification to household members that movie is starting

   - o Brief pause before beginning to allow for snack preparation

   - o Custom response like "The theater is now open, enjoy your movie!"

Genre-Specific Variations

Create multiple entertainment routines for different experiences:

- **Horror Movie Mode**: Deeper dimming with subtle red accent lighting

- **Sports Event**: Brighter lighting with team colors if possible

- **Gaming Setup**: Task lighting positioned to reduce screen glare

- **Music Listening**: Optimized audio settings with visualizer lighting if available

Advanced Automation

While voice control provides immediate interaction with your smart home, true automation operates independently, responding to schedules, sensors, and conditions without requiring your input. When combined with voice capabilities, these automated systems create a responsive environment that anticipates and adapts to your needs.

Time-Based Automation

Scheduling actions based on time provides a foundation for home automation:

Scheduling Fundamentals

- **Fixed Schedules**: Set actions to occur at specific times and days (e.g., lights on at 7:00 PM every day).

- **Relative Timing**: Schedule actions relative to sunrise and sunset, automatically adjusting throughout the year.

- **Offset Scheduling**: Set actions to occur before or after events (e.g., 30 minutes before sunset).

- **Random Variation**: Add slight randomness to scheduled events for more natural patterns and improved security.

Implementation Methods

For Amazon Alexa:

1. Create a routine with a scheduled trigger

2. Select time, recurrence pattern, and days of the week

3. Add actions to execute at the scheduled time

4. Optionally enable announcements from specific devices

For Google Assistant:

1. In the Google Home app, create a new routine

2. Select schedule as the starter

3. Define time, days, and which speaker should announce it

4. Add desired actions to the routine

Practical Applications

- **Morning Preparation**: Gradually increase lighting and adjust temperature before wake-up time

- **Work Hours**: Adjust home settings during predictable away periods

- **Evening Transitions**: Create lighting and temperature changes that signal the end of workday

- **Seasonal Adjustments**: Develop different schedules for different seasons

- **Vacation Simulation**: Create varied schedules that simulate occupancy while away

Sensor-Triggered Automation

Sensors add awareness to your smart home, allowing it to respond to environmental changes and human activity:

Sensor Types and Applications

- **Motion Sensors**: Trigger lighting, climate, or security changes based on presence detection

- **Contact Sensors**: Respond to doors or windows opening/closing

- **Temperature Sensors**: Adjust heating/cooling based on actual conditions in specific rooms

- **Light Sensors**: Modify lighting based on natural light levels

- **Humidity Sensors**: Control fans or dehumidifiers based on moisture levels

- **Water Sensors**: Alert and respond to potential leaks or flooding

Creating Sensor-Based Routines

Using Native Voice Assistant Features:

1. In your assistant's app, create a routine with a sensor change as the trigger

2. Select the specific sensor and state (e.g., motion detected, door opened)

3. Define actions to occur when triggered

4. Set optional conditions like time restrictions

Using Third-Party Automation Platforms: For more complex sensor integrations, consider platforms like:

- SmartThings

- Home Assistant

- Hubitat

- IFTTT

These platforms offer more sophisticated condition handling and device compatibility.

Advanced Sensor Strategies

- **Occupancy-Based Control**: Combine motion sensors with timers to determine true occupancy versus momentary movement

- **Multi-Sensor Logic**: Require multiple sensor conditions to trigger actions (e.g., motion AND low light levels)

- **Graduated Response**: Create different actions based on how long a condition exists

- **Zone-Based Automation**: Define areas of your home that operate semi-independently based on local sensors

- **Activity Recognition**: Use patterns of sensor activation to identify specific activities

Condition-Based Automation

Adding conditional logic creates smart home responses that adapt to multiple factors:

Condition Types

- **Environmental Conditions**: Temperature, humidity, air quality, or weather data

- **Device States**: Status of other smart devices (on/off, percentage, mode)

- **Time Windows**: Restricting actions to certain hours or days

- **User Presence**: Based on smartphone location or dedicated presence sensors

- **Usage Patterns**: Historical data about typical behavior

Creating Conditional Automations

While basic conditional logic is available in voice assistant platforms, more complex conditions typically require third-party automation platforms:

Using Voice Assistant Native Capabilities:

1. Create a routine with appropriate trigger

2. Add conditional parameters where available (typically time restrictions)

3. Test with various conditions to verify behavior

Using Dedicated Automation Platforms:

1. Select trigger events or conditions

2. Define conditional statements (IF-THEN-ELSE logic)

3. Create action sequences for each condition path

4. Add time-based or state-based conditions

Example: Smart Temperature Management

Create a comprehensive temperature management system:

1. **Base Trigger**: Schedule or occupancy detection

2. **Conditions**:

   - IF room temperature is already within 2 degrees of target, take no action

   - IF room is occupied AND temperature is outside comfort range, adjust immediately

   - IF room is unoccupied BUT expected to be occupied within 30 minutes, begin gradual adjustment

   - IF home is unoccupied AND expected to remain so for over 2 hours, maintain energy-saving temperature

3. **Actions**: Appropriate HVAC adjustments based on condition evaluation

Combining Voice Control with Automation

The true power of a smart home emerges when voice control and automation work together:

Integration Strategies

- **Voice Overrides**: Allow voice commands to temporarily override automated schedules

- **Duration Controls**: Include duration parameters in voice commands ("Alexa, turn on the living room lights for 30 minutes")

- **Mode Switching**: Use voice to change between different automation modes ("Hey Google, set vacation mode")

- **Status Queries**: Ask about automation status ("Alexa, when is the next scheduled event?")

- **Temporary Suspensions**: Pause automations with voice ("Hey Google, pause automations for two hours")

Advanced Integration Examples

Morning Flexibility:

- Routine normally runs at 6:30 AM on weekdays

- Voice command "Alexa, delay morning routine" pushes schedule back 30 minutes

- Voice command "Hey Google, I'm leaving early" triggers immediate execution of morning sequence

Presence Adaptation:

- Home automatically adjusts based on presence detection

- Voice command "Alexa, we have guests" modifies standard behaviors for visitor comfort

- Command "Hey Google, everyone's home" overrides normal occupancy detection for family gatherings

Automation Troubleshooting and Refinement

Even well-designed automations require adjustment and troubleshooting:

Common Issues and Solutions

- **Timing Problems**: If automations run at incorrect times, verify time zone settings and check for daylight saving time issues

- **Trigger Failures**: When automations don't start, confirm sensor battery levels and connectivity

- **Partial Execution**: If only some actions complete, look for device-specific connectivity issues

- **Conflicting Automations**: Identify and resolve routines that may be counteracting each other

- **Unwanted Activations**: Adjust sensor sensitivity or add conditions to prevent false triggers

Refinement Process

1. **Observe**: Document when automations work correctly and when they fail

2. **Analyze**: Look for patterns in failures (time of day, specific devices, network status)

3. **Modify**: Make small, incremental changes to address issues

4. **Test**: Verify improvements under various conditions

5. **Document**: Keep records of successful configurations for future reference

Troubleshooting Common Voice Control Problems

Even well-designed voice control systems occasionally encounter issues. Knowing how to diagnose and resolve these problems will ensure your smart home remains responsive and reliable.

Recognition and Response Issues

When voice assistants struggle to understand commands or respond incorrectly:

Diagnosis Steps

1. **Verify Wake Word**: Confirm the device is actually activating when you say the wake word.

2. **Check Indicator Lights**: Most assistants show visual feedback when listening.

3. **Test Simple Commands**: Try basic commands to isolate whether the problem is recognition or execution.

4. **Check Different Voices**: Have another household member try the same command.

5. **Review Command History**: Check the assistant's app to see what it thought you said.

Resolution Approaches

- **Retrain Voice Model**: Use voice training features if available to improve recognition.

- **Adjust Microphone Sensitivity**: Increase sensitivity if detection is the issue.

- **Modify Command Phrasing**: Try alternative wording that may be more recognizable.

- **Check for Interference**: Identify and eliminate sources of background noise.

- **Reposition Devices**: Move assistants away from noise sources or reflective surfaces.

- **Clean Microphones**: Ensure microphone openings aren't obstructed by dust or debris.

Connectivity Problems

Network issues frequently affect voice assistant performance:

Diagnostic Indicators

- Delayed responses to commands

- "I'm having trouble connecting to the internet" messages

- Device showing as offline in companion app

- Intermittent responsiveness

- Ability to hear commands but inability to execute smart home controls

Resolution Steps

1. **Verify Internet Connection**: Confirm other devices are connecting successfully.

2. **Check Wi-Fi Signal Strength**: Use the assistant's app to check connection quality.

3. **Restart Networking Equipment**: Power cycle your router and modem.

4. **Reduce Network Congestion**: Limit bandwidth-heavy activities when using voice control.

5. **Consider Wi-Fi Extenders**: Add mesh network nodes or range extenders if signal strength is the issue.

6. **Update Router Firmware**: Ensure your router is running the latest software.

7. **Separate 2.4GHz and 5GHz Networks**: Give them distinct names to ensure devices connect to the appropriate band.

Device Control Failures

When the assistant recognizes commands but fails to control smart devices:

Diagnostic Approach

1. **Verify Device Status**: Check if the device appears as connected in the assistant's app.

2. **Test Device Directly**: Attempt to control the device from its native app to isolate the issue.

3. **Check Multiple Devices**: Determine if the problem affects all devices or just specific ones.

4. **Review Recent Changes**: Consider if recent software updates or network changes preceded the issue.

Resolution Strategies

- **Reconnect Devices**: Remove and re-add problem devices to your voice assistant.

- **Update Device Firmware**: Check for updates in the device's native app.

- **Refresh Skills/Services**: Disable and re-enable the relevant integration in your assistant's app.

- **Check Naming Conflicts**: Ensure no two devices share the same or very similar names.

- **Verify Account Linkage**: Confirm that third-party accounts remain properly connected.

- **Factory Reset**: As a last resort, reset the problematic device and reconfigure it from scratch.

Routine Execution Problems

When automated routines fail to run properly:

Troubleshooting Process

1. **Check Individual Components**: Test each device in the routine independently.

2. **Verify Trigger Conditions**: Ensure that scheduling or sensor triggers are properly configured.

3. **Review Recent Changes**: Consider if routine modifications or device updates may have affected functionality.

4. **Examine Error Messages**: Look for specific error notifications in the assistant's app.

Fixing Routine Issues

- **Simplify to Isolate**: Temporarily remove actions from the routine to identify problematic components.

- **Recreate from Scratch**: Sometimes recreating the routine is faster than troubleshooting a complex one.

- **Check for Conflicts**: Ensure no other routines are counteracting the desired behavior.

- **Verify Device Limitations**: Some devices have restrictions on how frequently they can be controlled.

- **Add Delays**: Insert pauses between actions to prevent overloading devices or networks.

Privacy and Security Concerns

Addressing privacy issues ensures peace of mind with voice-enabled systems:

Common Privacy Issues

- Unintended activations mistaking conversation for wake words

- Uncertainty about what recordings are stored and for how long

- Concerns about who may have access to voice data

- Unauthorized purchases or actions through voice commands

Security and Privacy Enhancements

- **Review and Delete History**: Regularly clear voice history through the assistant's app or website.

- **Adjust Listening Settings**: Configure options regarding recording storage and review.

- **Enable Purchase Confirmations**: Require PIN codes for voice purchases.

- **Use Mute Functions**: Utilize physical mute buttons during sensitive conversations.

- **Configure Voice Recognition**: Set up voice matching to prevent unauthorized users from accessing personal data.

- **Regular Security Audits**: Periodically review connected accounts and authorized devices.

Advanced Troubleshooting Techniques

For persistent issues that resist standard troubleshooting:

Network Analysis

- **Device Isolation**: Connect voice assistant to a mobile hotspot to rule out home network issues.

- **Port Forwarding Check**: Verify that required ports aren't blocked by router settings.

- **Bandwidth Testing**: Use speed tests to ensure sufficient internet capacity.

- **IP Conflict Resolution**: Assign static IP addresses to critical smart home devices.

System Resets

When other methods fail, systematic reset approaches can resolve stubborn issues:

1. **Soft Reset**: Restart the voice assistant device.

2. **Factory Reset**: Return device to original settings (note: this requires complete reconfiguration).

3. **Infrastructure Refresh**: Systematically restart all network components from modem outward.

4. **Cache Clearing**: Clear app caches on mobile devices used to control the system.

5. **Account Refresh**: Log out and back into assistant accounts on all devices.

Manufacturer Support

When to escalate to professional help:

- After methodically attempting all self-service troubleshooting

- When multiple devices show similar issues suggesting a system-wide problem

- If hardware appears damaged or malfunctions in unusual ways

- When security concerns suggest possible unauthorized access

Maintaining Voice Assistant Performance

Preventative maintenance helps avoid future issues:

Regular Maintenance Practices

- **Update All Software**: Keep voice assistants, smart devices, and mobile apps updated.

- **Clean Physical Devices**: Periodically dust voice assistant devices, focusing on microphone areas.

- **Audit Connected Services**: Review and remove unused skills, services, and connected accounts.

- **Network Maintenance**: Regularly restart network equipment and update firmware.

- **Routine Testing**: Periodically verify that critical functions and routines still work as expected.

- **Documentation**: Maintain an updated list of devices, accounts, and successful configuration settings.

Anticipating Future Issues

Planning for potential problems ensures quicker resolution when they occur:

- **Backup Power**: Consider UPS (Uninterruptible Power Supply) for critical network and voice control components.

- **Offline Alternatives**: Maintain basic manual controls for essential functions.

- **Configuration Backups**: Where possible, export and save device settings and routines.

- **Staged Updates**: Avoid updating all devices simultaneously to limit widespread disruptions.

- **Change Management**: Document system changes to help identify the source of new issues.

By implementing these troubleshooting strategies and preventative measures, you'll ensure your voice-controlled smart home remains reliable and responsive. Remember that voice assistants and their ecosystems are constantly evolving, so occasional adjustments will be necessary as new features and capabilities become available.

Voice control represents one of the most intuitive and powerful interfaces for your smart home. With proper setup, thoughtful automation, and effective troubleshooting knowledge, you'll create a responsive environment that understands and anticipates your needs through the simple power of your voice.

Chapter 6: Home Automation for Energy Management

Overview of Smart Energy Management

Home automation has revolutionized many aspects of daily living, but perhaps its most practical and financially beneficial application lies in energy management. By leveraging smart technology to monitor and control your home's power consumption, you can significantly reduce waste, lower utility bills, and decrease your environmental footprint—all while maintaining or even improving comfort and convenience.

Smart energy management combines hardware, software, and thoughtful automation to create a home that uses only the energy it needs, when it needs it. This approach moves beyond simple energy conservation (using less) to energy optimization (using exactly what's needed, precisely when needed). The result is a home that conserves resources and saves money without sacrificing comfort or functionality.

This chapter explores the devices, systems, and strategies that can transform your home into an energy-efficient environment that responds dynamically to your needs and usage patterns while continuously working to minimize unnecessary consumption.

Energy-Saving Smart Devices

The foundation of automated energy management begins with smart devices specifically designed to control, monitor, and optimize power usage throughout your home. These devices range from simple plug-and-play solutions to more integrated systems that work together to create comprehensive energy management.

Smart Plugs and Outlets

Smart plugs represent the simplest entry point into energy management automation, offering immediate control over virtually any plugged-in device without requiring electrical work or significant technical knowledge.

Key Features and Capabilities

- **Remote Power Control**: Turn connected devices on or off from anywhere using smartphone apps

- **Energy Monitoring**: Track power consumption of individual devices in real-time and over time

- **Scheduling**: Create time-based on/off schedules for connected appliances

- **Usage Pattern Recognition**: Some advanced models learn device usage patterns and suggest optimization strategies

- **Voice Control Integration**: Compatible with voice assistants for hands-free operation

- **Surge Protection**: Many units include built-in surge protection to safeguard connected devices

- **Away Mode Simulation**: Randomly power devices on and off to simulate occupancy for security

Applications for Maximizing Savings

- **Phantom Power Elimination**: Control devices that consume standby power even when "off" (TVs, game consoles, computer equipment)

- **Timed Device Control**: Automatically power off frequently forgotten energy consumers (space heaters, curling irons, coffee makers)

- **Seasonal Appliance Management**: Easily manage seasonal items like holiday lights, pool pumps, or space heaters

- **Usage Limitation**: Restrict energy-intensive devices to specific hours (e.g., charging devices during off-peak rate periods)

- **Remote Verification**: Check and turn off forgotten devices after leaving home

Selection Considerations

- **Maximum Load Capacity**: Ensure the smart plug can handle the power requirements of intended devices (typically 10-15 amps)

- **Form Factor**: Choose compact designs that don't block adjacent outlets

- **Energy Monitoring Accuracy**: Consider models with more precise measurement capabilities if detailed tracking is important

- **Platform Compatibility**: Verify compatibility with your existing smart home ecosystem (HomeKit, SmartThings, etc.)

- **Connection Type**: Choose between Wi-Fi, Zigbee, Z-Wave, or Bluetooth based on your existing network infrastructure

Smart Power Strips

Smart power strips extend the functionality of individual smart plugs by controlling multiple devices simultaneously, often with added intelligence about how connected devices relate to each other.

Advanced Features

- **Master/Slave Outlets**: Automatically control secondary devices based on the power state of a primary device

- **Individual Outlet Control**: Separately program and control each outlet in the strip

- **Always-On Outlets**: Designate certain outlets to remain powered regardless of automation rules

- **Scheduling Per Outlet**: Set different schedules for each outlet

- **Surge Protection**: Protect sensitive electronics from power surges

- **Energy Monitoring**: Track power consumption by outlet or for the entire strip

Strategic Applications

- **Entertainment Centers**: Automatically power down accessory devices (game consoles, speakers, streaming devices) when the TV is turned off

- **Home Office Setup**: Turn off monitors, printers, and speakers when the computer is shut down

- **Charging Stations**: Schedule power only during needed hours to prevent overcharging and wasted electricity

- **Workshop/Garage**: Control power tools and equipment based on usage patterns and safety considerations

Smart Thermostats

Among smart home devices, thermostats typically offer the greatest energy-saving potential since **heating and cooling account for approximately 50% of home energy consumption in most climates.**

Energy-Saving Capabilities

- **Learning Algorithms**: Advanced models learn your preferences and patterns to automatically optimize settings

- **Geofencing**: Adjust temperature based on household members' locations to avoid heating or cooling an empty home

- **Smart Scheduling**: Create temperature programs based on daily routines, with different settings for weekdays and weekends

- **Remote Temperature Adjustment**: Change settings from anywhere using smartphone apps

- **Occupancy Detection**: Sense when people are home and adjust accordingly

- **Weather Responsiveness**: Monitor local weather forecasts to proactively adjust heating and cooling

- **Usage Reports**: Provide detailed analytics about energy consumption patterns

- **Maintenance Alerts**: Notify when system performance indicates potential issues or filter changes

Optimization Strategies

- **Setback Temperatures**: Automatically lower heating or raise cooling temperatures during sleep hours or away periods

- **Pre-heating/cooling**: Intelligently begin adjusting temperature before scheduled occupancy to maximize comfort while minimizing runtime

- **Fan Circulation Optimization**: Use the system fan to distribute air more effectively without running the heating or cooling components

- **Humidity Consideration**: Factor humidity levels into perceived comfort to avoid unnecessary system operation

- **Zoned Temperature Control**: When integrated with smart vents or zoned HVAC systems, target conditioning only to occupied areas

Installation Considerations

- **System Compatibility**: Verify compatibility with your existing HVAC system (conventional, heat pump, multi-stage, etc.)

- **C-Wire Requirements**: Determine if your system has the required common wire for powering the thermostat

- **Sensor Placement**: Position the thermostat away from drafts, sunlight, and heat-generating appliances for accurate readings

- **Multiple Thermostat Coordination**: For homes with multiple HVAC zones, ensure thermostats can communicate and coordinate operation

Smart Window Coverings

Often overlooked in energy management, automated window coverings can significantly reduce heating and cooling needs by controlling solar heat gain and retention.

Energy Management Features

- **Automated Positioning**: Adjust blinds or shades based on time, temperature, or sunlight conditions

- **Solar Tracking**: Follow the sun's position throughout the day to optimize light and heat

- **Temperature Responsiveness**: Close during peak heat hours in summer or open to capture solar heat in winter

- **Integration with HVAC**: Coordinate with thermostat to reduce heating/cooling load

- **Remote Control**: Adjust from anywhere via smartphone

- **Scene Compatibility**: Include in whole-home energy scenes (away mode, sleep mode, etc.)

Seasonal Strategies

- **Summer Configuration**: Close blinds on sun-facing windows during peak heat hours to reduce cooling needs

- **Winter Optimization**: Open blinds on south-facing windows during daylight hours to capture solar heat, close at night to retain warmth

- **Transition Season Programming**: Create specific automations for spring and fall to take advantage of natural temperature regulation

Smart Water Heaters

Water heating represents the second-largest energy expense in most homes, making it an excellent target for automation.

Smart Control Options

- **Timer Controllers**: Simple devices that control when the water heater operates

- **Smart Temperature Adjustment**: More advanced systems that modify temperature settings based on usage patterns

- **Usage Learning**: Track hot water consumption to predict needs and heat water only when necessary

- **Recirculation Control**: Manage hot water recirculation pumps to balance immediate availability with energy conservation

- **Leak Detection**: Monitor for potential water leaks to prevent damage and wasted energy

Optimization Approaches

- **Time-of-Use Scheduling**: Heat water during off-peak electricity rate periods

- **Vacation Mode:** Reduce or eliminate heating during away periods

- **Pre-Heating Strategy**: Learn household routines to ensure hot water is available exactly when needed

- **Integration with Smart Home Presence**: Respond to household members' arrivals and departures

Smart Lighting Systems

While individual energy savings may be modest, the ubiquity of lighting throughout the home makes it a significant cumulative target for energy management.

Energy-Efficient Components

- **LED Bulbs**: Base technology that uses 75-80% less energy than traditional incandescent bulbs

- **Smart Switches**: Control existing fixtures without replacing bulbs

- **Smart Bulbs**: Individual bulbs with wireless control capabilities

- **Occupancy Sensors**: Detect presence to automatically control lighting

- **Daylight Sensors**: Measure ambient light to adjust artificial lighting accordingly

Automation Strategies

- **Occupancy-Based Control**: Automatically turn lights off in unoccupied rooms

- **Daylight Harvesting**: Dim or turn off lights when sufficient natural light is available

- **Dimming Optimization**: Use only the minimum necessary brightness for different activities

- **Scheduling**: Create time-based controls for both indoor and outdoor lighting

- **Scene Integration**: Include lighting in whole-home energy scenes

- **Pathway Lighting**: Illuminate only necessary areas during nighttime hours rather than entire rooms

Setting Up Energy Monitoring

While automated control provides the mechanism for energy savings, comprehensive monitoring creates the intelligence needed to optimize those controls and verify the results. An effective energy monitoring system gives visibility into consumption patterns, identifies opportunities for improvement, and quantifies the savings achieved.

Whole-Home Energy Monitoring

Tracking total household energy consumption provides the broadest view of your usage patterns and the impact of your energy management strategies.

Monitoring Options

- **Smart Electric Panels**: Upgraded electrical panels with built-in monitoring for every circuit

- **Electric Meter Readers**: Devices that attach to your existing utility meter to capture consumption data

- **Current Transformer Systems**: Clamp-on sensors that measure electricity flowing through your main service lines

- **Utility-Provided Solutions**: Smart meters and monitoring programs offered by some electric companies

- **Solar Integration**: Energy monitoring features included with many solar panel installations

Implementation Process

1. **Select Appropriate Technology**:

   - For renters or those seeking non-invasive options: consider utility programs or non-permanent meter readers

   - For homeowners planning long-term: investigate panel upgrades or current transformer systems

   - For homes with solar: leverage existing monitoring and expand if necessary

2. **Installation Considerations**:

   - Current transformers typically require installation by a licensed electrician

   - Ensure proper placement and calibration of sensors

   - Verify Wi-Fi coverage at installation location

   - Consider battery backup to maintain monitoring during power outages

3. **Software Setup**:

   - Connect to home network and register with manufacturer's service

   - Set up user accounts for household members

- Configure alert thresholds for unusual consumption

- Integrate with other smart home platforms if applicable

4. **Baseline Measurement**:

- Allow system to collect data for at least one full week

- Include both weekday and weekend patterns

- Note seasonal factors that might affect the baseline

Using Whole-Home Data Effectively

- **Identify Base Load**: Determine your home's minimum power draw when supposedly "everything is off"

- **Recognize Usage Patterns**: Observe how consumption varies by time of day, day of week, and occupancy

- **Detect Anomalies**: Set up alerts for unusual consumption that might indicate malfunctioning equipment

- **Measure Improvement Impact**: Quantify the effect of energy-saving measures or device replacements

- **Correlate with External Factors**: Connect consumption patterns with weather data, occupancy, or activities

Device-Level Monitoring

While whole-home monitoring provides the big picture, device-level tracking identifies specific opportunities for optimization and allows targeted automation strategies.

Monitoring Methods

- **Smart Plugs with Energy Tracking**: Easiest implementation for individual plug-in devices

- **Circuit-Level Monitoring**: Track major appliances or rooms that have dedicated electrical circuits

- **Device-Specific Systems**: Use manufacturer-provided monitoring for major appliances

- **Smart Appliances**: Leverage built-in consumption reporting in newer appliances

- **Distributed Sensor Networks**: Deploy multiple monitors throughout the home for comprehensive coverage

High-Value Monitoring Targets

- **Refrigeration**: Often among the largest constant energy consumers

- **HVAC System**: Break out heating and cooling from overall consumption

- **Water Heater**: Track patterns to optimize heating schedules

- **Entertainment Systems**: Identify phantom power issues and usage patterns

- **Home Office Equipment**: Quantify work-related energy consumption

- **Laundry Appliances**: Monitor energy and potential water usage

- **Kitchen Appliances**: Track major energy users like ovens and dishwashers

Data Analysis Strategies

- **Consumption Ranking**: Identify the largest energy consumers to prioritize optimization efforts

- **Usage Pattern Identification**: Determine when and how devices are being used

- **Efficiency Comparison**: Compare similar devices to identify less efficient models

- **Phantom Power Detection**: Measure standby power consumption

- **Degradation Tracking**: Watch for increasing energy usage that might indicate maintenance needs

- **Behavioral Correlation**: Connect energy usage to specific household activities and habits

Setting Up a Monitoring Dashboard

Transforming collected data into actionable information requires effective visualization and analysis tools.

Dashboard Elements

- **Real-Time Consumption Display**: Current power draw for the whole home and major components

- **Historical Comparison Views**: Compare today's usage with previous days, weeks, or months

- **Cost Calculation**: Convert kilowatt-hours to actual dollars based on utility rate structures

- **Goal Tracking**: Visualize progress toward energy reduction targets

- **Device Breakdown**: Show percentage of consumption by device or category

- **Peak Usage Identification**: Highlight periods of highest consumption

- **Environmental Impact**: Calculate carbon footprint or equivalent metrics

Implementation Options

- **Manufacturer Ecosystems**: Use the dashboard provided by your monitoring system manufacturer

- **Third-Party Platforms**: Connect your devices to services like Home Assistant, Hubitat, or SmartThings

- **Custom Solutions**: For technically inclined users, create personalized dashboards using platforms like Grafana or Node-RED

- **Multi-System Integration**: Combine data from different monitoring systems into a unified view

Effective Dashboard Configuration

- **Placement**: Position displays in frequently viewed locations or make them easily accessible on mobile devices

- **User-Specific Views**: Create different dashboards for various household members based on their interests or responsibilities

- **Alert Configuration**: Set up notifications for unusual conditions or achievement of goals

- **Information Hierarchy**: Organize from most important/actionable information to detailed analysis

- **Action Shortcuts**: Include direct controls for major energy-consuming devices

DIY Project: Smart Plug Deployment Strategy

One of the most accessible and effective energy management projects involves strategically deploying smart plugs throughout your home. This project guides you through the process of identifying optimal locations, selecting appropriate devices, and configuring them for maximum energy savings.

Planning Your Smart Plug Strategy

Before purchasing devices, develop a comprehensive plan to ensure you target the highest-value opportunities.

Energy Audit Process

1. **Inventory Plug-In Devices**:

- List all plugged-in items throughout your home
- Note which ones remain plugged in but unused for extended periods
- Identify devices known to draw significant standby power

2. **Prioritize Control Opportunities:**

- Devices frequently left on accidentally
- Equipment with high phantom power draw
- Appliances that could safely operate on schedules
- Seasonal items that need occasional control

3. **Consider Usage Patterns:**

- Daily use versus occasional use items
- Devices used on regular schedules
- Equipment needing remote verification (was it left on?)
- Appliances that should operate during specific rate periods

4. **Group Control Possibilities:**

- Entertainment center components
- Home office equipment
- Charging stations

- Seasonal or occasional use devices

Device Selection Criteria

- **Individual Smart Plugs**: Best for standalone devices located away from other controlled items

- **Smart Power Strips**: Ideal for clusters of related devices

- **Outdoor-Rated Models**: Required for exterior holiday lighting, pool equipment, etc.

- **High-Capacity Versions**: Necessary for power-hungry appliances

- **Energy Monitoring Features**: Most valuable for understanding consumption of specific devices

Implementation Guide: Entertainment Center

Follow this step-by-step process to optimize energy use in a typical home entertainment setup.

Required Materials

- Smart power strip with master/slave functionality

- Smartphone with manufacturer's app

- Optional: voice assistant device for integration

Setup Process

1. **Identify Components**:
   - Categorize devices as primary (TV, receiver) or secondary (game console, streaming device, speakers)

- Note typical usage patterns and which devices are commonly left on

2. **Physical Installation**:
   - Disconnect all devices from existing power
   - Connect primary device (typically TV) to the master outlet
   - Connect secondary devices to controlled outlets
   - Connect always-on devices (cable boxes, DVRs) to uncontrolled outlets if needed

3. **App Configuration**:
   - Create device groups and labels for easy identification
   - Configure power thresholds for master device detection
   - Set appropriate shut-off delay times for secondary devices

4. **Testing and Tuning**:
   - Verify master device detection works reliably
   - Adjust sensitivity if necessary
   - Test that all secondary devices power down appropriately
   - Check for any devices that need special handling

5. **Usage Monitoring**:

    o Track energy consumption for at least one
      week

    o Compare to previous consumption if data
      is available

    o Identify additional optimization
      opportunities

Implementation Guide: Home Office

Create an energy-efficient workspace that eliminates
wasteful consumption without disrupting productivity.

Required Materials

- Smart plugs (individual or power strip,
  depending on setup)

- Optional: occupancy sensor

- Smartphone with control app

Setup Process

1. **Analyze Work Patterns**:

    o Identify regular work hours

    o Note which equipment is needed
      constantly versus occasionally

    o Consider which devices can be safely
      powered down during breaks

2. **Device Classification**:

- Always-on devices (routers, security equipment)

- Work-hours-only devices (monitors, printers, speakers)

- As-needed devices (scanners, chargers, task lighting)

3. **Physical Installation**:

   - Install smart plugs for each category of equipment

   - Position any sensors to accurately detect workspace occupancy

   - Ensure easy access to manual controls if needed

4. **Automation Configuration**:

   - Set core business hours for automated power

   - Create "starting work" and "ending work" routines

   - Configure manual triggers for easy activation

5. **Schedule Refinement**:

   - Observe actual usage versus planned schedules

   - Adjust automation timing to match actual work patterns

o   Add special rules for weekends or variable schedules

Implementation Guide: Seasonal Equipment

Create flexible controls for devices used only during specific times of the year.

Required Materials

- Weather-appropriate smart plugs (indoor or outdoor)
- Optional: temperature sensors
- Smartphone with control app

Setup Process

1. **Identify Seasonal Equipment:**

   o   Holiday lighting and decorations

   o   Portable heaters or fans

   o   Pool or garden equipment

   o   Seasonal entertainment items (projectors, outdoor speakers)

2. **Installation Considerations:**

   o   Use outdoor-rated equipment for exterior applications

   o   Consider physical protection from elements

   o   Ensure adequate WiFi coverage at installation locations

3. **Configuration Approaches:**

- Calendar-based activation periods
- Temperature-triggered operation
- Sunset/sunrise scheduling
- Manual activation with automatic shut-off

4. **Testing and Safety Verification**:
   - Confirm remote control functions properly
   - Verify automatic shut-off features work reliably
   - Check for appropriate load handling

5. **Documentation**:
   - Record seasonal configurations for easy reactivation
   - Note any special considerations for future reference

Automated Power Management

Beyond simply controlling individual devices, comprehensive energy management involves creating coordinated automation systems that intelligently manage your home's power consumption based on occupancy, time, activities, and external factors.

Occupancy-Based Power Management

One of the most effective automation strategies involves adjusting energy usage based on whether spaces are actually occupied.

Detection Methods

- **Motion Sensors**: Detect movement within spaces

- **Contact Sensors**: Monitor door openings and closings

- **Presence Detection**: Use smartphone location or dedicated presence sensors

- **Network Presence**: Track devices connecting to home network

- **Intelligent Algorithms**: Combine multiple data points to determine true occupancy versus temporary absence

Automation Strategies

- **Immediate Response**: Turn off non-essential devices when rooms become unoccupied

- **Delayed Action**: Implement countdown timers for potential brief absences

- **Graduated Response**: Apply increasingly aggressive power-saving measures as vacant time increases

- **Return Preparation**: Begin restoring optimal conditions shortly before expected return

- **Occupancy Patterns**: Learn and anticipate typical household movements

Implementation Examples

1. **Living Room Automation**:

- Lights, entertainment system, and fans turn off 10 minutes after no motion is detected

- Smart plugs disconnect power to eliminate phantom draw after 30 minutes

- Climate settings adjust to energy-saving levels after 60 minutes

- Upon detecting renewed occupancy, restore preferred settings

2. **Whole-Home Vacancy Response**:

- When all presence sensors indicate no occupants, initiate "Away" mode

- Power down non-essential systems completely

- Set remaining systems to minimum necessary operation

- Adjust security features as needed

- Monitor for return of any household member

Time-Based Energy Automation

Schedule-based automation ensures efficient operation aligned with household routines and utility rate structures.

Scheduling Frameworks

- **Fixed Time Schedules:** Set specific hours for device operation

- **Relative Time Triggers**: Schedule relative to sunrise, sunset, or other events

- **Rate-Aware Timing**: Align energy-intensive operations with lower-cost periods

- **Adaptive Scheduling**: Automatically adjust timing based on changing patterns

- **Sequential Coordination**: Stagger high-draw device operation to avoid demand spikes

Rate Optimization Techniques

- **Time-of-Use Strategies**: Shift flexible loads to lower-rate periods

- **Demand Charge Avoidance**: Prevent multiple high-consumption devices from operating simultaneously

- **Critical Peak Pricing Response**: Automatically reduce consumption during utility peak events

- **Real-Time Pricing Adaptation**: Adjust usage based on current electricity prices

- **Load Shifting**: Move energy-intensive activities away from peak periods

High-Value Applications

1. **Electric Vehicle Charging:**

   - Schedule charging during lowest rate periods

   - Ensure completion before needed departure times

o   Adjust based on battery level and urgency

2. **Water Heating Management**:

   o   Heat water primarily during off-peak hours

   o   Maintain minimum comfortable temperatures during peak periods

   o   Temporarily boost for specific needs (showers, dishwasher cycles)

3. **Thermal Storage Optimization**:

   o   Pre-cool or pre-heat home during favorable rate periods

   o   Utilize thermal mass to maintain comfort during rate transitions

   o   Balance comfort requirements with cost optimization

Activity-Based Energy Management

Beyond occupancy and schedules, truly intelligent energy management responds to specific activities occurring within the home.

Activity Detection Methods

- **Device State Combinations**: Recognize patterns of multiple devices operating together

- **Voice Assistant Integration**: Use voice commands as activity indicators

- **Direct Selection**: Allow users to indicate current activities through apps or controls

- **Sensor Fusion**: Combine multiple sensor inputs to infer activities
- **Machine Learning**: Develop recognition of complex patterns over time

Energy-Optimized Activity Modes

1. **Movie Watching**:
   - Dim or turn off lights except minimal bias lighting
   - Adjust HVAC for optimal comfort during extended seated activity
   - Power down unnecessary devices in the viewing area
   - Optimize audio and display equipment for efficiency

2. **Cooking Sessions**:
   - Provide task lighting while minimizing other kitchen lighting
   - Ensure proper ventilation while managing HVAC interaction
   - Preheat appliances precisely when needed rather than prematurely
   - Adjust refrigerator cycles to avoid competing with cooking appliances

3. **Sleep Mode**:
   - Progressively power down common areas

- Optimize bedroom conditions for sleep (temperature, humidity)

- Maintain minimal essential systems

- Schedule morning preparation in advance

Weather-Responsive Energy Management

External conditions significantly impact energy needs, making weather-based automation an essential component of comprehensive energy management.

Weather Data Integration

- **Local Weather Services**: Connect to online forecast providers

- **Personal Weather Stations**: Install home weather monitoring equipment

- **Predictive Algorithms**: Anticipate needs based on upcoming conditions

- **Historical Pattern Analysis**: Compare current conditions to past experiences

- **Seasonal Adjustments**: Modify baselines based on time of year

Automation Applications

1. **Temperature-Based Adjustments**:

   - Modify heating and cooling setpoints based on outdoor conditions

   - Adjust operation of ceiling fans and air circulation

- Control supplemental heating or cooling in problem areas

2. **Solar Gain Management:**
   - Automate window coverings based on sun position and intensity
   - Leverage passive solar heating during cool weather
   - Block excessive heat gain during warm periods

3. **Humidity Response:**
   - Coordinate dehumidification during humid conditions
   - Manage humidification during dry periods
   - Balance ventilation with energy efficiency

4. **Storm Preparation:**
   - Automatically enter energy-conservation mode during power outage risks
   - Manage battery backup systems in anticipation of utility disruptions
   - Protect sensitive equipment from potential power quality issues

Cost Savings Over Time

While the primary goal of energy management automation is reducing consumption, the financial impact provides tangible, measurable benefits that justify the investment in smart home technology.

Calculating Energy Savings

Understanding the financial impact of your energy management system requires accurate measurement and analysis of both energy reduction and cost implications.

Measurement Approaches

- **Before-and-After Comparison**: Compare utility bills from similar periods before and after implementation

- **Weather-Normalized Analysis**: Account for temperature differences between comparison periods

- **Device-Specific Calculation**: Measure actual consumption changes for individual devices

- **Utility Data Integration**: Utilize detailed data available from smart meters and utility portals

- **Control Group Comparison**: Compare with similar properties without energy management systems

Savings Calculation Methods

1. **Direct Energy Reduction**:
   - Calculate kilowatt-hour reduction
   - Multiply by appropriate rate tiers
   - Account for time-of-use rate differences

2. **Demand Charge Impact:**

   o Identify peak demand reduction

   o Apply utility-specific demand charge rates

   o Calculate monthly and annual impact

3. **Equipment Lifespan Extension:**

   o Estimate reduced run hours for major equipment

   o Calculate extended replacement intervals

   o Determine annual depreciation benefit

4. **Maintenance Reduction:**

   o Quantify reduced maintenance frequency

   o Calculate labor and parts savings

   o Include convenience value of fewer disruptions

Sample Cost Analysis: Smart Thermostat

This example illustrates the typical financial impact of implementing a smart thermostat with proper automation in a moderate climate.

Assumptions

- Average home size: 2,000 square feet

- Pre-installation annual HVAC cost: $1,500

- Smart thermostat cost with installation: $250

- Typical optimization achievable: 15% reduction

First-Year Financial Impact

- Energy cost reduction: $225 (15% of $1,500)
- Installation investment: $250
- Net first-year impact: -$25 (payback nearly complete in year one)

Five-Year Impact

- Cumulative energy savings: $1,125
- Potential utility rebates: $50-$100
- Extended equipment life value: ~$125
- Total five-year benefit: ~$1,300
- Return on investment: Approximately 520%

Sample Cost Analysis: Comprehensive Energy Management

This analysis examines the financial impact of implementing a complete energy management system including monitoring, smart plugs, automated lighting, and HVAC control.

Assumptions

- Average home with $2,400 annual electricity cost
- Comprehensive system investment: $1,200
- Implementation focused on highest-impact opportunities
- System expanded gradually over one year

Projected Savings by Category

- Phantom power elimination: 5-8% ($120-$192)
- HVAC optimization: 10-15% ($240-$360)
- Lighting automation: 3-5% ($72-$120)
- Major appliance management: 4-7% ($96-$168)
- Total potential reduction: 22-35% ($528-$840)

Long-Term Financial Analysis

- First-year net savings: -$360 to -$672 (accounting for installation costs)
- Second-year net savings: $528-$840
- Five-year cumulative savings: $2,352-$3,600
- Ten-year cumulative savings: $5,280-$8,400
- Simple payback period: 1.5-2.3 years

Beyond Direct Energy Savings

The financial benefits of energy management systems extend beyond simple utility cost reduction.

Additional Financial Benefits

- **Equipment Lifespan Extension**: Reduced runtime and optimized operation extend the useful life of major appliances and HVAC equipment
- **Maintenance Reduction**: Fewer operating hours typically translate to less frequent maintenance requirements

- **Peak Demand Avoidance**: For utilities with demand charges, significant savings from reduced peak consumption

- **Time-of-Use Optimization**: Automatically shifting consumption to lower-rate periods

- **Problem Identification**: Early detection of failing or inefficient equipment before major failures occur

- **Property Value Enhancement**: Growing evidence that smart energy features increase home resale value

Environmental and Comfort Benefits

While more difficult to quantify financially, these additional benefits contribute to overall return on investment:

- **Carbon Footprint Reduction**: Lower energy consumption directly reduces environmental impact

- **Improved Comfort Control**: More precise management of home environment

- **Convenience Value**: Reduced need to manually adjust and monitor systems

- **Peace of Mind**: Remote monitoring and control while away from home

- **Data-Driven Decisions**: Better information for future home improvement investments

Maximizing Financial Return

Strategic approaches can help ensure you achieve the greatest possible return on your energy management investment.

Investment Prioritization

1. **Start with No-Cost Measures**:
   - Adjust existing device settings for efficiency
   - Develop energy-conscious household behaviors
   - Utilize manual scheduling of current equipment

2. **Low-Investment, High-Return Implementations**:
   - Smart plugs for phantom power control
   - Basic smart thermostat installation
   - LED lighting conversion

3. **Strategic System Expansion**:
   - Add monitoring to identify next-priority targets
   - Implement room-by-room control where most beneficial
   - Address seasonal energy challenges

4. **Comprehensive Integration**:
   - Develop coordinated whole-home automation

- o Implement advanced occupancy-based controls

- o Create activity-specific energy modes

Utility Program Participation

Many utilities offer programs that can enhance the financial benefits of energy management:

- **Rebate Programs**: Direct reimbursement for purchasing qualified smart devices

- **Demand Response**: Compensation for allowing utility to temporarily adjust consumption during grid stress

- **Time-of-Use Rate Opt-In**: Access to lower rates during off-peak hours

- **Home Efficiency Programs**: Free or discounted energy audits and improvements

- **Solar Integration Incentives**: Additional benefits for homes with renewable generation

Continuous Optimization Strategies

The greatest long-term financial benefits come from ongoing refinement of your energy management system:

- **Regular Performance Review**: Monthly assessment of energy consumption and costs

- **Seasonal Adjustments**: Update automation rules to match changing weather patterns

- **New Technology Integration**: Strategically incorporate improved devices as they become available

- **Behavior Adjustment**: Fine-tune systems to match evolving household activities and schedules

- **Data Analysis**: Use accumulated energy data to identify remaining optimization opportunities

Building a Sustainable Smart Home

Energy management represents the intersection of smart home convenience and practical financial benefit. By thoughtfully implementing the devices, systems, and strategies outlined in this chapter, you can create a home that not only responds to your needs but does so while minimizing environmental impact and reducing ongoing costs.

The most successful energy management implementations share several key characteristics:

- **Incremental Implementation**: Starting with high-impact opportunities and gradually expanding

- **User-Centric Design**: Creating systems that enhance rather than complicate daily living

- **Measurable Outcomes**: Establishing clear metrics for success and tracking progress

- **Continuous Improvement**: Treating energy management as an ongoing process rather than a one-time project

- **Balanced Approach**: Finding the optimal point between conservation and convenience

As you continue your smart home journey, remember that energy management automation isn't just about saving money—it's about creating a home that uses resources intelligently, responds to your needs efficiently, and contributes to a more sustainable future while enhancing your quality of life.

Chapter 7: Building a Smart Garden

Introduction to Smart Gardens

The concept of gardening has evolved significantly in recent years, moving beyond traditional manual cultivation to embrace technological innovations that enhance efficiency, sustainability, and enjoyment. A smart garden integrates technology to automate routine tasks, monitor environmental conditions, and optimize plant growth with minimal human intervention. This marriage of horticulture and technology offers benefits for gardeners of all experience levels, from novices seeking to avoid common pitfalls to experienced enthusiasts looking to perfect their craft.

Smart gardens address several fundamental challenges faced by traditional gardening approaches:

Water Conservation: Traditional irrigation methods often lead to water waste through evaporation, runoff, or simply applying more water than plants require. Smart irrigation systems can reduce water usage by 20-50% by delivering precise amounts of water exactly when and where needed, based on real-time soil conditions and weather forecasts.

Time Efficiency: Maintaining a garden traditionally

requires consistent attention and manual labor. Automated systems handle routine tasks like watering and lighting, freeing gardeners to focus on more enjoyable aspects like planning and harvesting.

Plant Health Optimization: Many plant problems stem from inconsistent care or failure to notice early warning signs. Smart sensors can detect subtle changes in soil moisture, nutrition, temperature, and light levels before visible symptoms appear, enabling proactive intervention.

Seasonal Adaptability: Garden needs change dramatically with seasons, requiring constant adjustments to watering schedules and care routines. Smart systems can automatically adapt to seasonal changes and weather patterns without manual reprogramming.

The evolution of smart garden technology has made these systems increasingly accessible to homeowners:

First Generation: Simple timers for irrigation and lighting that operated on fixed schedules regardless of conditions.

Second Generation: Programmable systems with basic sensors that could adjust operations based on limited environmental data.

Current Technology: Fully integrated systems with advanced sensors, weather integration, smartphone control, and machine learning capabilities that truly adapt to your garden's specific needs.

Smart gardens can be implemented at various scales:

Container Gardens: Even apartment dwellers with balcony plants can benefit from self-watering containers with built-in sensors.

Small Residential Gardens: Suburban homes with limited garden space can implement targeted smart irrigation zones and basic monitoring.

Large Landscapes: Extensive properties can utilize comprehensive systems with multiple zones, detailed environmental tracking, and integrated management of various garden elements.

When planning your smart garden, consider both immediate needs and future expansion. Many gardeners begin with a single smart component—often irrigation—and gradually add functionality as they become comfortable with the technology and identify additional needs. This modular approach allows for budget-friendly implementation while building toward a comprehensive system.

Required Equipment: Smart Irrigation Systems, Sensors, Smart Garden Lights

Creating a functional smart garden requires thoughtful selection of key components that work together as an integrated system. Each element serves a specific purpose in the automation and monitoring of your garden environment.

Smart Irrigation Systems

The foundation of most smart gardens is an intelligent watering system that delivers precise amounts of water based on actual plant needs rather than rigid schedules.

Controller Hubs:

- **Smart Controllers**: These replace traditional irrigation timers, connecting to Wi-Fi for weather data integration and smartphone control. Leading options include Rachio, Orbit B-hyve, and RainMachine.
- **Features to Consider**: Weather integration, zone-specific controls, flow meters for leak detection, EPA WaterSense certification, compatibility with home automation platforms.
- **Installation Complexity**: Most replace existing irrigation controllers with similar wiring but add smart capabilities.

Distribution Systems:

- **Drip Irrigation**: Delivers water directly to plant roots with minimal waste. Components include pressure regulators, filters, tubing, emitters, and micro-sprayers.
- **Smart Sprinklers**: For lawns and larger areas, these feature precision spray patterns and sometimes individual head control.

- **Smart Hose Attachments**: Budget-friendly options that add intelligence to existing garden hoses.

Advanced Features:

- **Flow Sensors**: Detect leaks or blockages by monitoring water usage patterns.
- **Master Valves**: Automatically shut off water supply when leaks are detected.
- **Rain/Freeze Sensors**: Prevent watering during precipitation or freezing conditions.

Environmental Sensors

These devices monitor crucial environmental factors that affect plant health and system efficiency.

Soil Moisture Sensors:

- **Types**: Capacitive sensors (more accurate, longer-lasting) vs. resistive sensors (more affordable, less durable).
- **Placement**: Typically installed at root depth of target plants, with different sensors for different garden zones.
- **Connectivity**: Wireless sensors communicate with the irrigation controller to trigger watering only when soil moisture drops below target levels.
- **Popular Options**: ECOWITT, Govee, Spruce, and sensors integrated with irrigation controllers.

Weather Stations:

- **Functions**: Measure rainfall, temperature, humidity, wind speed, and solar radiation.
- **Benefits**: Adjust irrigation based on evapotranspiration rates and actual rainfall.
- **Integration**: Many connect with irrigation controllers and home automation systems.
- **Options**: Range from simple rain gauges to comprehensive stations from Davis Instruments, Ambient Weather, or Netatmo.

Specialized Plant Sensors:

- **Nutrient Monitors**: Measure soil EC (electrical conductivity) to indicate fertilizer levels.
- **pH Sensors**: Monitor soil acidity/alkalinity for optimal nutrient uptake.
- **Light Meters**: Ensure plants receive appropriate light intensity and duration.
- **All-in-One Options**: Products like Scotts Gro, Gardena, or Xiaomi Plant Monitors combine multiple measurements in one device.

Smart Garden Lights

Outdoor lighting enhances garden aesthetics while providing practical benefits for security and usability.

Pathway and Accent Lighting:

- **Solar Options**: Self-contained units that charge during daylight and illuminate at night.

- **Low-Voltage Systems**: Wired lights connected to transformers, offering more consistent illumination.
- **Smart Features**: Adjustable brightness, color temperature, and timing control.
- **Popular Brands**: Philips Hue Outdoor, LIFX, Ring, Govee, and Kasa Outdoor.

Security Lighting:

- **Motion-Activated Fixtures**: Trigger illumination when movement is detected.
- **Scheduled Security**: Simulate presence with variable timing patterns.
- **Integration**: Connect with security cameras and home automation for coordinated response.

Specialized Horticultural Lighting:

- **Grow Lights**: Extend growing seasons with supplemental lighting for plants.
- **Timing Controls**: Automate day/night cycles for optimal plant growth.
- **Spectrum Adjustments**: Some systems offer variable light spectrum to promote different stages of plant growth.

Control and Integration Systems

These components tie individual elements together into a cohesive system:

Smart Home Hubs:

- **Platforms**: *Apple HomeKit, Amazon Alexa, Google Home, Samsung SmartThings.*
- **Functions**: Create routines that coordinate multiple devices based on time, sensors, or user input.
- **Considerations**: Ensure all garden components are compatible with your chosen platform.

Dedicated Garden Controllers:

- **All-in-One Systems**: Products like Gardena Smart System or Orbit B-hyve that integrate irrigation, sensing, and sometimes lighting.
- **Benefits**: Designed specifically for garden applications with appropriate weather resistance and specialized functions.

Smartphones and Applications:

- **Control Interface**: Most systems offer apps for configuration, monitoring, and manual control.
- **Notifications**: Alert users to unusual conditions or maintenance requirements.
- **Data Logging**: Track environmental conditions and system performance over time.

When budgeting for your smart garden, prioritize components based on your specific needs. For most gardens, a quality smart irrigation controller with basic moisture sensing capability provides the greatest immediate benefit and water savings. Additional components can be added incrementally as budget allows and as you identify specific requirements for your garden.

Step-by-Step Setup: Setting Up Irrigation Systems for Automated Watering

Installing a smart irrigation system is the cornerstone of an automated garden. This process transforms traditional manual watering into a precise, efficient operation that responds to actual plant needs and environmental conditions.

Planning Your System

Before purchasing components, thorough planning ensures your system meets your garden's specific requirements:

1. Create a Garden Map:
   - Sketch your garden layout, identifying different planting areas
   - Mark existing water sources and electrical outlets
   - Note areas with different watering needs (lawn, vegetable garden, shade plants, etc.)
   - Identify microclimates (areas that are particularly sunny, shady, windy, etc.)
2. Analyze Water Requirements:
   - Group plants with similar watering needs into zones
   - Consider soil types which affect water retention (clay, loam, sand)

- o Identify slopes that may affect water distribution
- o Note sun exposure patterns across your garden
3. Calculate System Capacity:
    - o Measure water pressure at your outdoor faucet (using a pressure gauge)
    - o Determine water flow rate (gallons per minute) by timing how long it takes to fill a 5-gallon bucket
    - o Check that your water source can support your planned system
4. Select Distribution Method for each zone:
    - o Drip irrigation: For individual plants, containers, vegetable gardens
    - o Micro-sprayers: For ground covers and densely planted beds
    - o Traditional sprinklers: For lawns and larger areas
    - o Soaker hoses: For row plantings or hedges

Installing a Smart Irrigation Controller

The controller is the brain of your system, making decisions about when and how much to water:

1. Remove Existing Controller (if applicable):
    - o Take a photo of current wiring before disconnection
    - o Turn off power at the breaker
    - o Label wires according to their zones
    - o Detach the old controller from the wall

2. Install Smart Controller:
   - Mount in a protected location with access to power and Wi-Fi
   - For outdoor installation, ensure the controller has appropriate weather protection
   - Connect zone wires to corresponding terminals (following your photo or labels)
   - Connect common wire (usually white) to the common terminal
   - Install any included weather sensors (rain, freeze)
3. Configure Power and Network:
   - Connect power supply
   - Turn on breaker
   - Follow manufacturer instructions to connect to your home Wi-Fi network
4. Set Up Controller Software:
   - Download the manufacturer's app on your smartphone
   - Create an account and register your device
   - Follow guided setup to input:
     - Your location for local weather data
     - Plant types in each zone
     - Soil types
     - Sprinkler head types (if applicable)
     - Sun exposure for each zone
     - Slope characteristics

Installing Distribution System

With the controller in place, now set up the physical

components that deliver water to your plants:

For Drip Irrigation Zones:

1. **Install Backflow Preventer** at the water source to prevent contamination of household water
2. **Add Pressure Regulator** to reduce water pressure to appropriate levels (typically 25-30 PSI for drip systems)
3. **Connect Filter** to prevent clogging of small emitters and tubing
4. **Install Main Line:**
   - Use 1/2" or 3/4" polyethylene tubing as your main supply line
   - Run from water source through garden, following planned routes
   - Secure with landscape stakes every 3-5 feet
   - Add manual shut-off valves for maintenance sections
5. **Connect Zone Valves** to main line at points where separate control is needed:
   - Connect valve wires to corresponding controller terminals
   - Ensure valves are installed in the correct orientation (note flow direction arrows)
   - Place valves in valve boxes for protection and accessibility
6. **Add Distribution Tubing:**
   - Connect 1/4" distribution tubing to main lines using appropriate fittings

- Run tubing to individual plants or planting areas
- Install emitters:
  - 1 GPH (gallon per hour) for small plants
  - 2 GPH for medium shrubs
  - 4+ GPH for large plants and trees
- Multiple emitters for larger plants, spaced around the drip line
7. **Install End Caps and Flush Valves** at the end of each main line

For Sprinkler Zones:

1. **Connect Valves** to main water supply and controller
2. **Install Sprinkler Pipes:**
   - Dig trenches 6-12" deep depending on freeze potential in your region
   - Lay PVC or poly pipe according to your design
   - Connect to valves using appropriate fittings
3. **Install Sprinkler Heads:**
   - Choose appropriate heads for each area (rotary, fixed, bubbler)
   - Ensure consistent coverage with appropriate overlap
   - Adjust spray patterns to avoid watering sidewalks or structures
4. **Add Smart Flow Meter** (optional but recommended):

- Install between water source and main system
- Connect to controller following manufacturer instructions
- Configure leak detection thresholds

Testing and Calibration

Proper testing ensures efficient operation and identifies potential issues:

1. Perform Initial Pressure Test:
   - Close all end caps and valves
   - Pressurize system
   - Check for leaks at connections
2. Flush the System:
   - Remove end caps
   - Run each zone for 2-3 minutes to flush debris
   - Replace end caps
3. Test Each Zone Individually:
   - Check coverage patterns
   - Verify all emitters or sprinklers are functioning
   - Adjust heads as needed for proper coverage
4. Install and Calibrate Moisture Sensors:
   - Place sensors at root depth of representative plants in each zone
   - Avoid areas with unusual drainage
   - Connect to controller according to manufacturer instructions

- Set moisture thresholds based on plant types
5. Configure Smart Features:
   - Enable weather integration
   - Set water restrictions if applicable to your region
   - Configure notifications for system issues
   - Set seasonal adjustments or enable automatic adjustment

Programming Your System

Modern smart controllers minimize the need for detailed programming, but initial setup establishes baseline operation:

1. Set Watering Windows:
   - Morning hours (4-7 AM) typically ideal to minimize evaporation and fungal issues
   - Avoid evening watering when possible (promotes disease)
   - Comply with any local water restrictions
2. Configure Zones:
   - Define basic parameters for each zone based on plant types
   - Set initial run times as a starting point
   - Enable smart watering features that adjust based on weather and soil moisture
3. Create Special Schedules for:
   - Newly planted areas (requiring more frequent watering)
   - Seasonal plants with changing needs

   o Establishment periods for trees and shrubs
4. Set Up Alerts and Monitoring:
   o Enable notifications for abnormal conditions
   o Configure usage reports
   o Set maintenance reminders
5. Document Your System:
   o Create a map showing valve, sensor, and main line locations
   o Record zone settings and plant requirements
   o Store component manuals and reference information

After initial setup, monitor your system closely for the first few weeks, making adjustments as needed. The true advantage of smart irrigation comes from its ability to learn and adapt over time, becoming increasingly efficient as it collects data about your specific garden conditions.

Monitoring Plant Health: Using Smart Sensors for Soil Moisture and Temperature

The key to successful gardening often lies in understanding what's happening below the surface. Smart sensors transform invisible soil conditions into actionable data, allowing for precise interventions before plants show visible signs of stress.

Understanding Soil Monitoring Fundamentals

Before deploying sensors, it's important to understand

the key metrics they track and why they matter:

Soil Moisture: The amount of water present in soil exists in three states:

- **Gravitational Water**: Excess water that drains away
- **Available Water**: Moisture plants can access (the ideal target range)
- **Unavailable Water**: Moisture bound too tightly to soil particles for plants to use

Most plants thrive when soil moisture is maintained between 40-60% of field capacity, though specific requirements vary by species.

Soil Temperature: Affects seed germination, nutrient availability, root growth, and microbial activity:

- Below 50°F (10°C): Limited root growth and nutrient uptake
- 50-65°F (10-18°C): Good for cool-season plants
- 65-85°F (18-29°C): Optimal for most plants
- Above 85°F (29°C): Stressful for many plants, especially in combination with dry conditions

Soil Nutrition: Measured through electrical conductivity (EC) as a proxy for available nutrients:

- Too low: Plants may suffer nutrient deficiencies
- Too high: Can cause root burn and nutrient toxicity

Soil pH: Affects nutrient availability and microbial activity:

- 5.5-7.0: Optimal range for most garden plants
- Below 5.5: Too acidic for many plants; limits availability of many nutrients
- Above 7.0: Too alkaline; limits availability of iron, manganese, and phosphorus

Deploying Soil Sensors Effectively

Strategic placement and proper installation ensure that sensors provide meaningful data:

1. **Choose Appropriate Sensor Types:**
   - **Capacitive moisture sensors**: More accurate and durable than resistive types
   - **Temperature probes**: Should be corrosion-resistant for long-term use
   - **pH/EC sensors**: Generally require occasional calibration
2. **Determine Optimal Placement:**
   - Install at the effective root depth of target plants (typically 4-12" depending on plant type)
   - Place in representative locations, not in unusually wet or dry spots
   - For large areas, use multiple sensors to account for soil variations
   - Avoid placing directly adjacent to irrigation emitters (creates false readings)
   - For container gardens, use sensors specifically designed for pots

3. **Installation Best Practices:**
    o Soak the sensor in water before installation (unless manufacturer advises otherwise)
    o Create a pilot hole with a soil probe rather than forcing sensors into dry soil
    o Ensure good soil contact around all sensing elements
    o For wireless sensors, verify adequate signal strength before finalizing placement
    o Mark sensor locations with small flags for easy identification
4. **Establish Baseline Readings:**
    o Record initial readings when soil is known to be at ideal moisture levels
    o Document readings under various conditions (after rain, during hot periods, etc.)
    o Note differences between morning and afternoon readings

Creating a Comprehensive Monitoring System

Individual sensors become more valuable when integrated into a coordinated monitoring approach:

1. **Set Up Sensor Network:**
    o Connect sensors to your smart controller or hub following manufacturer instructions
    o Name each sensor according to location or plant group it monitors

- Verify consistent communication between all components
2. Configure Thresholds and Alerts:
    - Set moisture thresholds based on specific plant needs:
        - Drought-tolerant plants: Allow to dry more between watering
        - Moisture-loving plants: Maintain higher consistent moisture
    - Create temperature alerts for extreme conditions:
        - Frost warnings for tender plants
        - High-temperature alerts during heatwaves
    - Enable notifications for out-of-range conditions
3. Integrate with Weather Data:
    - Connect system to local weather forecasts through your controller or hub
    - Configure predictive responses (e.g., skip watering when rain is predicted)
    - Enable seasonal adjustments based on temperature trends
4. **Establish Data Logging:**
    - Set up automatic recording of sensor readings
    - Review trends weekly during the first growing season
    - Identify patterns that inform better garden management

Interpreting and Acting on Sensor Data

The true value of monitoring comes from using the collected data to optimize plant care:

1. Learn to Read Moisture Patterns:
   - Observe how quickly different areas dry out after watering
   - Note seasonal changes in moisture retention
   - Identify areas that may need soil amendments to improve water retention
2. Respond to Temperature Data:
   - Add mulch to moderate soil temperature extremes
   - Time planting and harvesting based on soil temperature trends
   - Protect sensitive plants when soil temperatures approach critical thresholds
3. Address Nutrition Fluctuations:
   - Correlate EC readings with plant performance
   - Time fertilization based on nutrient depletion patterns
   - Avoid fertilizing when plants are under moisture stress
4. Create Automation Rules Based on Sensor Input:
   - Trigger supplemental watering only when moisture falls below target levels
   - Adjust irrigation run times based on actual soil moisture depletion
   - Pause scheduled irrigation when moisture levels remain adequate
5. Document and Refine:

- Keep records of plant performance in relation to sensor readings
- Note successful interventions for future reference
- Adjust sensor thresholds based on observed plant responses

Advanced Plant Monitoring Technologies

Beyond basic soil sensors, several emerging technologies offer deeper insights into plant health:

Sap Flow Sensors: Directly measure water movement through plant stems, providing the most accurate picture of plant water usage.

Dendrometers: Track minute changes in stem diameter to detect early signs of water stress before visible wilting occurs.

Spectral Analysis: Specialized cameras that detect changes in leaf coloration invisible to the human eye, identifying nutrient deficiencies or disease before symptoms are visible.

Environmental Stations: Monitor ambient conditions (light, humidity, air temperature) alongside soil factors for comprehensive understanding of plant stress factors.

While these technologies are becoming more accessible to home gardeners, they represent the next frontier in precision gardening. Starting with quality soil moisture and temperature monitoring provides the foundation upon which more advanced systems can later be built.

Remember that even the most sophisticated sensors serve as tools to inform—not replace—thoughtful gardening practices. The data they provide should complement your observations and knowledge of your specific plants and growing conditions.

Smart Garden Lights: Automating Outdoor Lighting for Aesthetics and Security

Strategic lighting transforms a garden from a daytime-only space into a round-the-clock environment that enhances property aesthetics, extends usable hours, and provides crucial security benefits. Smart lighting technology adds automation, energy efficiency, and creative possibilities that conventional lighting cannot match.

Types of Smart Garden Lighting

Modern outdoor lighting systems offer specialized fixtures for different purposes:

Pathway Lighting:

- **Purpose**: Illuminates walkways for safety and navigation
- **Smart Features**: Motion activation, brightness adjustment based on ambient light

- **Placement**: Staggered 6-8 feet apart along paths, mounted 18-24 inches high
- **Options**: Bollard lights, mushroom lights, downward-facing path lights

Accent Lighting:

- **Purpose**: Highlights landscape features, plants, or architectural elements
- **Smart Features**: Color changing, scene setting, scheduling
- **Techniques:**
    - Uplighting: Illuminating from below to highlight trees or structures
    - Silhouetting: Placing lights behind objects to create dramatic outlines
    - Grazing: Positioning lights at steep angles to emphasize texture
- **Options**: Spotlights, well lights, wash lights

Security Lighting:

- **Purpose**: Deters intruders, illuminates potential hazards
- **Smart Features**: Motion detection, remote activation, integration with security systems
- **Placement**: Entry points, blind corners, property perimeters
- **Options**: Flood lights, motion-sensor fixtures, integrated camera lights

Ambient/Entertainment Lighting:

- **Purpose**: Creates atmosphere for outdoor gathering spaces
- **Smart Features**: Color synchronization with music, scene creation, remote control
- **Placement**: Decks, patios, pergolas, outdoor kitchens
- **Options**: String lights, tape lights, lanterns, color-changing fixtures

Planning Your Smart Lighting System

Effective outdoor lighting begins with thoughtful planning:

1. Identify Lighting Zones based on function:
   - Safety zones (steps, level changes, hazards)
   - Security zones (entry points, vulnerable areas)
   - Feature zones (specimen plants, water features, sculptures)
   - Activity zones (dining areas, play spaces)
2. Conduct a Nighttime Assessment:
   - Walk your property after dark with a flashlight
   - Identify naturally dark areas that feel unsafe
   - Note special features that would benefit from highlighting
   - Consider views from inside the house
3. Map Electrical Access:
   - Note existing outdoor outlets

- Identify potential locations for transformers
- Consider solar options for areas distant from power
- Plan cable routes that can be concealed
4. Select Control Technology:
   - Wi-Fi systems for comprehensive integration
   - Bluetooth for simpler, localized control
   - Proprietary RF systems for reliability
   - Hub-based systems for complex automation
5. Consider Light Characteristics:
   - Color temperature (measured in Kelvins):
     - Warm white (2700-3000K): Natural, inviting for living spaces
     - Neutral white (3500-4000K): Crisp, good for task areas
     - Cool white (5000K+): High visibility, best for security
   - Brightness (measured in lumens):
     - Paths: 100-200 lumens
     - Accent: 80-300 lumens
     - Security: 700+ lumens
   - Beam spread:
     - Narrow (15-30°): For highlighting specific features
     - Medium (40-60°): For general illumination
     - Wide (60-120°): For washing walls or broader areas

Installation Process

Installing smart garden lighting requires attention to both aesthetic and technical considerations:

1. Prepare the Infrastructure:
   - For low-voltage systems:
     - Install transformer near power source
     - Run main cables along planned routes
     - Bury cables 3-6 inches deep or conceal under mulch
     - Use conduit for areas vulnerable to damage
   - For solar systems:
     - Ensure panels receive at least 6 hours of direct sunlight
     - Position control units for optimal sun exposure
     - Consider separate solar collectors if fixture locations are shaded
   - For Wi-Fi systems:
     - Verify outdoor Wi-Fi coverage in all lighting areas
     - Install range extenders if necessary
     - Position hub in protected location with good signal
2. Install Fixtures Methodically:
   - Begin with pathway lighting for basic navigation
   - Add security lighting at key points

- Install accent lighting for featured elements
- Complete with ambient lighting for living spaces

3. For Each Fixture:
   - Position temporarily before permanent installation
   - Test effect at night and adjust as needed
   - Secure firmly to prevent shifting
   - Connect to main cable using waterproof connectors
   - Conceal wiring with landscape elements

4. Connect to Control System:
   - Follow manufacturer instructions to add devices to your network
   - Name each light or group logically (e.g., "Front Path," "Oak Tree Accent")
   - Test remote control functionality before finalizing placement
   - Update firmware if required

Creating Smart Lighting Automations

The true potential of smart garden lighting emerges through thoughtful automation:

1. Basic Scheduling:
   - **Sunset/Sunrise Triggers**: Set lights to activate automatically at dusk and deactivate at dawn
   - **Time-Based Control**: Program specific on/off times for different zones

- Seasonal Adjustments: Create separate schedules for different seasons or automatically adjust to changing daylight hours
2. Security Automations:
   - Vacation Mode: Simulate occupancy with varied lighting patterns
   - Motion Response: Trigger brightness increase when motion is detected
   - Integration with Security System: Coordinate lighting with alarm events
   - Geofencing: Activate welcome lighting when you approach home
3. Sensor-Based Control:
   - Light Level Detection: Adjust brightness based on natural light conditions
   - Weather Response: Increase illumination during foggy or stormy conditions
   - Motion Efficiency: Activate pathway lighting only when someone is present
4. Entertainment Features:
   - Scene Creation: Design preset configurations for different activities (dining, parties, relaxation)
   - Color Changing: Program seasonal color themes or special event lighting
   - Music Synchronization: Coordinate light pulses with outdoor audio
   - Voice Control: Enable commands through smart assistants
5. Integration with Other Garden Systems:

- Irrigation Coordination: Illuminate active water features during irrigation cycles
- Weather Station Response: Adjust lighting based on current conditions
- Security Camera Enhancement: Ensure adequate illumination for night recording

Energy Efficiency Considerations

Smart lighting can significantly reduce energy consumption through intelligent control:

1. **Use LED Technology** exclusively for outdoor fixtures:
    - 80-90% more efficient than incandescent lighting
    - Lifespan of 15,000-50,000 hours reduces replacement frequency
    - Low voltage options improve safety
2. Implement Brightness Control:
    - Run lights at 60-80% brightness for normal conditions
    - Increase to 100% only when needed for activities or security
    - Dim to 30-40% for late night hours
3. Utilize Motion Activation strategically:
    - Maintain low background illumination for aesthetics
    - Increase brightness only when areas are in use
    - Return to baseline after preset duration of inactivity

4. Consider Solar Options where appropriate:
   - Best for accent and pathway lighting
   - Less reliable for security applications
   - Requires battery backup for consistent performance
   - Most effective in sunny climates

Maintenance and Troubleshooting

Even the best smart lighting systems require periodic attention:

1. Regular Physical Maintenance:
   - Clean fixture lenses quarterly to maintain light output
   - Reposition fixtures that shift due to ground movement
   - Trim vegetation that may block light or solar panels
   - Inspect for water intrusion or connection corrosion
2. System Maintenance:
   - Update control software and firmware when available
   - Replace batteries in battery-backed components
   - Test automation routines seasonally
   - Verify network connectivity periodically
3. Common Issues and Solutions:
   - Connectivity Drops:
     - Check Wi-Fi signal strength in problem areas

- Consider mesh network extensions
- Verify transformer and power supply function
  - Fixture Failure:
    - Test power at the fixture location
    - Inspect for water damage
    - Verify connections at transformer and fixture
    - Check for voltage drop on long cable runs
  - Automation Inconsistency:
    - Confirm accurate location settings
    - Check that time zones are set correctly
    - Verify sensor operation
    - Update automation rules for seasonal changes

Building a smart garden represents a perfect fusion of nature and technology—enhancing the beauty and productivity of your outdoor space while reducing resource consumption and maintenance requirements. The systems described in this chapter create a foundation that can evolve with your gardening skills and interests, allowing incremental expansion as you become more comfortable with the technology.

The core benefit of smart garden technology is not replacing the gardener but amplifying their capabilities. These systems handle routine tasks with precision while providing unprecedented insight into the previously invisible world of soil conditions and plant responses. This allows you to focus your attention on the creative and enjoyable aspects of gardening rather than mundane maintenance.

As you implement your smart garden, remember that technology should serve your gardening goals rather than define them. Start with the elements that address your most pressing challenges—whether that's consistent irrigation, monitoring problem areas, or enhancing outdoor living spaces with lighting. Build from this foundation as you identify additional needs or as your garden evolves.

The environmental benefits of smart gardening extend beyond your property boundaries. Water conservation through precision irrigation, reduced chemical use through targeted application, and energy efficiency through smart lighting collectively contribute to more sustainable landscaping practices. Your smart garden not only creates a more beautiful and enjoyable space but also serves as a model for responsible resource management.

The journey toward a fully automated garden is ongoing, with new technologies continually emerging. The systems you implement today create the infrastructure upon which future innovations can build, ensuring that your investment remains relevant as smart gardening continues to evolve. By embracing these technologies, you're not just creating a garden for today but establishing a dynamic, responsive environment that will continue to delight and sustain for years to come.

Chapter 8: Troubleshooting and Maintenance

How to Troubleshoot Your Smart Home Devices

In the world of smart home technology, encountering occasional issues is inevitable. The good news is that many common problems have simple solutions that you can implement yourself. Before calling technical support or replacing devices, try these troubleshooting steps:

The Universal Fix: Restart

It may sound cliché, but turning a device off and back on again resolves a surprising number of smart home issues. This simple action clears temporary memory, reestablishes connections, and resets software to a stable state.

1. Power cycle the device by unplugging it, waiting 30 seconds, then plugging it back in
2. For battery-operated devices, remove the batteries for 30 seconds before reinserting them
3. For app-related issues, force-close the app and restart it, or restart your smartphone

Connection Problems

Connectivity issues are among the most common problems in smart homes. If devices show as "offline" or "unavailable":

- Check your Wi-Fi router to ensure it's operating correctly
- Verify the device is within range of your Wi-Fi network or hub
- Confirm your internet service is active by checking other online devices
- Reset your router by unplugging it for 30 seconds and plugging it back in
- For Zigbee, Z-Wave, or Bluetooth devices, verify the hub or bridge is powered on and connected

Voice Assistant Troubleshooting

When voice assistants like Alexa, Google Assistant, or Siri aren't responding:

- Verify the device has power and an active internet connection
- Check that the microphone isn't muted (look for indicator lights)
- Try rephrasing your command using simpler, clearer language
- Move closer to the device to ensure it can hear you clearly
- Check for active timers or alarms that might be interfering

Smart Lighting Issues

For smart bulbs, switches, or lighting systems that aren't responding:

- Verify the physical switch controlling power to the light is turned on
- Check that the bulb is properly screwed in or that the switch has power
- Remove and reinstall the device from your smart home app
- Reset the bulb or switch according to manufacturer instructions
- For color-changing bulbs with incorrect colors, try factory resetting them

Smart Lock Problems

When smart locks fail to lock or unlock properly:

- Check the battery level and replace batteries if they're low
- Ensure the door is properly aligned with the frame
- Clean the lock mechanism to remove any dust or debris
- Verify that the lock's physical components move freely without resistance
- Recalibrate the lock following the manufacturer's instructions

Camera and Doorbell Troubleshooting

For issues with security cameras or video doorbells:

- Check power supply and battery levels
- Verify Wi-Fi connection strength at the device location
- Clean the camera lens to ensure clear visibility
- Adjust motion detection sensitivity to reduce false alerts
- Check storage settings for cloud recording or local storage

Temperature and HVAC Control Issues

When smart thermostats aren't properly controlling your climate:

- Verify that HVAC systems have power and are operational
- Check wiring connections at the thermostat
- Confirm that the thermostat is properly calibrated
- Ensure appropriate temperature thresholds are set
- Verify scheduling hasn't overridden manual settings

App and Software Issues

For problems with smart home apps:

- Check for app updates in your device's app store
- Clear the app's cache or data in your phone settings
- Uninstall and reinstall the app as a last resort
- Verify you're logged into the correct account

- Check for system-wide outages on the manufacturer's website

Maintenance Tips for Long-Term Use

Regular maintenance ensures your smart home devices operate efficiently and extends their lifespan. Implementing these practices will help prevent issues before they arise and keep your smart home running smoothly.

Regular Cleaning

Dust and debris can affect sensor performance and cause overheating:

- Gently dust cameras, speakers, and display screens monthly
- Use compressed air to clean ports and vents on hubs and controllers
- Wipe down touch interfaces with microfiber cloths to prevent buildup
- For outdoor devices, remove dirt, pollen, and other environmental debris
- Clean fingerprint sensors on smart locks to maintain reliable operation

Battery Management

Many smart home devices rely on batteries, which require attentive management:

- Replace batteries promptly when low-battery notifications appear
- For rechargeable devices, follow manufacturer recommendations for charging cycles
- Use high-quality batteries in battery-powered devices
- Remove batteries from seasonal devices during extended periods of non-use
- Keep spare batteries on hand for critical devices like door locks and security sensors

Environmental Considerations

The physical environment significantly impacts smart device performance:

- Maintain appropriate temperature ranges for devices (typically 32-95°F or 0-35°C)
- Keep humidity between 30-50% to prevent condensation and electrical issues
- Position devices away from direct sunlight to prevent overheating
- Shield outdoor devices from extreme weather conditions
- Ensure adequate ventilation around devices that generate heat

Routine Check-Ups

Proactive inspection helps identify potential issues before they become critical:

- Perform monthly visual inspections of wiring, connections, and physical condition
- Test backup batteries in security systems and smoke detectors
- Verify that automations and routines are functioning as expected
- Check that schedules and timers remain accurate, especially after power outages
- Inspect mounting hardware for cameras and outdoor devices to ensure stability

Network Maintenance

Your smart home is only as reliable as your network:

- Position your router centrally to provide even coverage throughout your home
- Regularly restart your router (monthly is recommended)
- Consider mesh networking solutions for larger homes
- Create a dedicated IoT network for your smart devices to enhance security
- Monitor network traffic to identify bandwidth issues or unauthorized devices

Data Management

Smart homes generate substantial data that requires occasional management:

- Review and delete old recordings from security cameras

- Clear logs and history data that may slow down system performance
- Regularly backup custom configurations and automation routines
- Review privacy settings and data sharing permissions
- Manage cloud storage accounts to ensure sufficient space for new recordings

Seasonal Adjustments

As seasons change, your smart home may require adjustments:

- Update thermostat schedules for seasonal temperature changes
- Adjust lighting automations to account for changing daylight hours
- Modify irrigation controllers based on seasonal precipitation patterns
- Recalibrate motion detection sensitivity for outdoor cameras as vegetation changes
- Review energy usage patterns and optimize accordingly

When to Call a Professional: Knowing When It's Time for an Expert

While many smart home issues can be resolved with DIY troubleshooting, some situations warrant professional assistance. Recognizing these scenarios can save time, prevent further damage, and ensure your safety.

Electrical Issues

Smart home components that interface with your electrical system may require professional attention:

- Problems with hardwired smart switches or outlets that persist after basic troubleshooting
- Installation of new hardwired devices if you lack electrical experience
- Flickering lights or circuit breaker trips when smart devices are in use
- Signs of electrical damage like scorching, burning smells, or melted components
- Upgrading electrical panels to accommodate additional smart home devices

Structural Integration Challenges

When smart technology meets building materials, specialized knowledge may be necessary:

- Installation of smart thermostats in complex HVAC systems
- Integration of smart blinds, shades, or curtain systems
- Mounting heavy equipment like large displays or projectors
- Installation of smart water valves or leak detection systems that require plumbing modifications
- Smart door locks that don't properly align with existing door frames

Network Infrastructure Problems

Persistent connectivity issues often require networking expertise:

- Dead zones in Wi-Fi coverage that basic troubleshooting can't resolve
- Setting up complex mesh networks for larger properties
- Creating segregated networks for enhanced smart home security
- Diagnosing interference issues between different wireless protocols
- Enterprise-level network configurations for extensive smart home installations

System Integration Complexities

When multiple systems need to work together seamlessly:

- Integration of disparate platforms that lack native compatibility
- Setting up complex, cross-platform automation sequences
- Implementing whole-home audio or video distribution systems
- Configuring advanced scene controls that span multiple subsystems
- Programming custom functionality beyond app capabilities

Security System Issues

For matters concerning your home's security:

- Integration of smart security with professional monitoring services
- Configuration of advanced camera systems with specialized mounting requirements
- Setting up comprehensive security zones with multiple sensor types
- Troubleshooting false alarms that persist despite basic adjustments
- Integration of smart security with existing traditional security systems

When to Consult with Specialists

Different types of professionals serve different smart home needs:

- **Electricians**: For hardwired devices, electrical panel upgrades, and power distribution
- **Systems Integrators**: For whole-home automation and complex multi-platform installations
- **Network Technicians**: For solving persistent connectivity issues and network optimization
- **HVAC Specialists**: For smart thermostats connected to complex heating/cooling systems
- **Security Professionals**: For integration with monitored security services
- **Custom Installers**: For aesthetically pleasing installations that integrate with décor

Cost-Benefit Considerations

Before hiring a professional, consider:

- The value of your time versus the cost of professional services
- The risk of damage to expensive components or home infrastructure
- Warranty implications of DIY versus professional installation
- The complexity of the task and your comfort level with technology
- Long-term reliability needs, especially for security-related systems

Firmware and Software Updates: Keeping Devices Up-to-Date

Regular updates are essential for optimal performance, security, and functionality of your smart home ecosystem. Understanding how to manage updates effectively ensures your devices remain current without causing disruptions.

Understanding Update Types

Different updates serve different purposes:

- **Firmware Updates**: Low-level software that controls device hardware functions
- **Software Updates**: Application-level improvements to features and interfaces
- **Security Patches**: Critical fixes for vulnerabilities that could be exploited

- **Feature Updates**: New capabilities or enhancements to existing functionality
- **Bug Fixes**: Corrections for known issues or performance problems

Update Strategies

Consider these approaches to managing updates:

- **Automatic Updates**: Configure devices to update automatically when possible, ideally during low-usage hours
- **Scheduled Updates**: Set specific times for updates to minimize disruption
- **Staged Updates**: Update less critical devices first to identify potential issues before updating essential systems
- **Notification-Based**: Receive alerts about available updates but apply them manually after reviewing change notes
- **Critical-Only**: For stable environments, focus on security updates while deferring feature updates

Best Practices for Updates

Follow these guidelines for smoother update experiences:

- Create backups of configurations before applying major updates
- Check manufacturer release notes to understand what's changing

- Update controllers and hubs before updating their dependent devices
- Ensure stable power and internet connections during update processes
- Keep devices at compatible firmware versions if they need to work together

Troubleshooting Update Issues

When updates don't go as planned:

- For failed updates, try resetting the device and attempting the update again
- If a device becomes unresponsive after an update, perform a factory reset as a last resort
- Contact manufacturer support for specific recovery procedures if available
- Look for rollback options to previous firmware versions if provided
- Check community forums for solutions to common update problems

Managing Updates Across Ecosystems

Multi-platform smart homes require coordinated update management:

- Create an inventory of devices with their current firmware versions
- Develop a schedule that updates related devices together
- Test integrations after updating one platform that connects with others

- Document successful update procedures for future reference
- Stay informed about upcoming major updates that might affect compatibility

When to Delay Updates

Sometimes, waiting before updating is the wiser choice:

- When traveling or during critical usage periods
- If the current system is working flawlessly for mission-critical applications
- When early adopters report issues with a new update
- If the update removes features you actively use
- When updates require reconfiguration of complex automations

Long-Term Support Considerations

Be mindful of manufacturer support lifecycles:

- Research manufacturer track records for long-term device support
- Consider the lifespan of devices with limited update support
- Plan for eventual replacement of devices that reach end-of-support status
- Evaluate subscription services that promise continued software updates
- Balance the benefits of newer hardware against the effort of migration

Security Maintenance: Keeping Your Smart Home Secure from Hacks

As your home becomes smarter, maintaining robust security becomes increasingly important. Regular security maintenance helps protect your privacy, prevents unauthorized access, and secures your personal data.

Regular Password Management

Strong password practices form your first line of defense:

- Change default passwords immediately upon device setup
- Use unique, complex passwords for each device and account
- Implement a password manager to track and generate strong credentials
- Enable two-factor authentication (2FA) wherever available
- Update passwords regularly, at least every 6-12 months
- Avoid sharing credentials across multiple platforms or services

Network Security

Your home network requires special attention:

- Separate IoT devices onto their own network or VLAN when possible

- Change the default SSID (network name) and password on your router
- Enable WPA3 encryption if supported, or at minimum WPA2
- Disable WPS (Wi-Fi Protected Setup) features that can be exploited
- Apply router firmware updates promptly
- Consider a dedicated firewall appliance for larger installations
- Regularly check for and remove unrecognized devices from your network

Device Vetting and Management

Not all smart devices are created equal in terms of security:

- Research manufacturer security practices before purchasing
- Favor devices from companies with strong security track records
- Regularly audit all connected devices and remove those no longer in use
- Disable unnecessary features and services that expand attack surfaces
- Check device privacy settings to minimize data collection and sharing
- Consider the security implications of devices with cloud dependencies

Physical Security

Don't overlook the physical aspects of smart home

security:

- Secure hubs, controllers, and network equipment in locations not easily accessible to visitors
- Consider tamper-resistant mounting for outdoor cameras and sensors
- Use privacy shutters or covers for cameras when not in use
- Position indoor cameras and microphones to minimize capturing sensitive areas
- Implement physical backup methods (like traditional keys) for critical systems like locks

Update Vigilance

Security-focused update practices are essential:

- Prioritize security patches over feature updates
- Subscribe to manufacturer security bulletins and alerts
- Monitor security news for vulnerabilities in devices you own
- Consider replacement for devices no longer receiving security updates
- Verify the authenticity of update sources before installation

Access Control Management

Control who has access to your systems:

- Regularly review and revoke access for individuals who no longer need it
- Use temporary access codes for service personnel rather than sharing primary credentials
- Implement role-based access with limited privileges for non-primary users
- Log out of smart home apps on devices you don't regularly use
- Review access logs periodically to identify suspicious activity

Data Protection

Smart homes generate valuable data that requires protection:

- Understand what data your devices collect and where it's stored
- Delete old recordings, logs, and history data regularly
- Review and limit data sharing with third parties
- Consider local storage solutions instead of cloud-only options when possible
- Back up configuration data securely to expedite recovery if needed

Incident Response Planning

Prepare for potential security breaches:

- Document steps to take if you suspect a device has been compromised

- Know how to perform factory resets on all your devices
- Create a security recovery checklist for quickly securing compromised systems
- Keep contact information for device manufacturers and support readily available
- Consider cyber insurance for high-value smart home installations

Continuous Security Education

Stay informed about emerging threats and defenses:

- Follow security blogs and news sources focused on IoT security
- Join user communities for your specific devices to learn about security considerations
- Understand common attack vectors like credential stuffing and firmware exploitation
- Evaluate new security technologies and approaches as they become available
- Share security best practices with other members of your household

By implementing these troubleshooting techniques, maintenance routines, and security practices, you'll ensure your smart home remains reliable, efficient, and secure for years to come. Remember that a proactive approach to maintenance and security will save time and frustration compared to reactive troubleshooting, and will ultimately provide a better smart home experience.

Conclusion and Next Steps

Recap of What You've Built

Congratulations on embarking on your smart home journey! Throughout this guide, you've transformed your living space into an interconnected ecosystem that responds to your needs, preferences, and habits. Let's take a moment to appreciate what you've accomplished:

Foundation Systems

You've established the critical infrastructure that serves as the backbone of your smart home:

- **Wi-Fi Network**: Optimized for coverage, speed, and reliability to handle multiple connected devices
- **Hub or Controller**: Selected based on your specific needs, whether it's a dedicated smart home hub, voice assistant, or smartphone app
- **User Accounts**: Created secure accounts across various platforms while implementing strong password practices
- **Home Layout**: Mapped your home's zones and identified the optimal locations for different types of devices

Core Functionalities

You've implemented fundamental smart home capabilities that enhance your daily life:

- **Lighting Control**: Installed smart bulbs, switches, or plugs that allow for remote control, scheduling, and automation of your home's lighting
- **Climate Management**: Set up smart thermostats and sensors that optimize comfort while potentially reducing energy costs
- **Security Systems**: Deployed cameras, smart locks, and sensors that keep your home and loved ones safe
- **Entertainment Integration**: Connected audio/video equipment for streamlined media experiences across your home

Automation and Intelligence

You've moved beyond basic remote control to create a truly "smart" environment:

- **Scenes and Routines**: Created preset configurations that adjust multiple devices simultaneously for specific activities or moods
- **Sensor-Based Automation**: Implemented systems that respond automatically to environmental changes, presence detection, or time-based triggers

- **Voice Control**: Integrated voice assistants that respond to natural language commands for hands-free operation
- **Mobile Access**: Set up remote access capabilities that allow you to monitor and control your home from anywhere

System Cohesion

You've unified disparate systems into a cohesive whole:

- **Cross-Platform Integration**: Connected devices from different manufacturers to work together through compatible standards or bridge devices
- **User Interfaces**: Customized dashboards, apps, and voice commands that provide intuitive control for all users
- **Failure Safeguards**: Implemented backup systems and manual overrides that ensure functionality even when technology falters
- **Privacy Protections**: Established boundaries that protect your data while still enabling the convenience of connected living

Maintenance Protocols

You've developed habits that ensure long-term reliability:

- **Troubleshooting Procedures**: Learned systematic approaches to diagnosing and resolving common issues

- **Update Management**: Created routines for keeping firmware and software current
- **Security Practices**: Implemented ongoing security measures that protect your smart home ecosystem
- **Regular Check-ups**: Established maintenance schedules that prevent problems before they occur

Your smart home is now more than a collection of gadgets—it's an integrated system that enhances your lifestyle, security, comfort, and efficiency. The fundamentals you've mastered provide a solid platform from which you can continue to refine, expand, and personalize your smart home experience.

Advanced DIY Smart Home Projects

With your solid foundation in place, you're well-positioned to explore more sophisticated projects that further customize your smart home to your unique preferences and needs. These advanced projects build upon your existing knowledge while introducing new skills, technologies, and capabilities.

Environmental Monitoring Systems

Create a comprehensive environmental monitoring network:

- **Air Quality Sensors**: Deploy sensors that detect particulate matter, VOCs, CO_2, and humidity levels throughout your home

- **Custom Dashboard**: Build a wall-mounted display that provides real-time environmental data visualization
- **Remediation Automation**: Configure systems to automatically activate air purifiers, exhaust fans, or HVAC fresh air intake based on sensor readings
- **Seasonal Trending**: Implement data logging to track environmental patterns over time and adjust systems seasonally
- **Alert Thresholds**: Create custom notifications for when specific environmental parameters exceed healthy ranges

Advanced Lighting Projects

Elevate your lighting beyond basic control:

- **Circadian Rhythm Lighting**: Program lights to automatically adjust color temperature throughout the day to match natural sunlight patterns and support healthy sleep cycles
- **Presence-Aware Lighting Paths**: Create sequential lighting that follows movement through your home by linking multiple motion sensors with intelligent timing
- **Scene Layering**: Design complex lighting scenes that combine ambient, task, and accent lighting with the ability to adjust individual components
- **Outdoor Landscape Integration**: Extend your smart lighting to gardens, pathways, and

architectural features with weather-aware controls

- **Art-Responsive Lighting**: Create systems that adjust lighting based on what's being displayed on TVs or digital art frames

Energy Management Systems

Optimize your home's energy usage with advanced monitoring and control:

- **Circuit-Level Power Monitoring**: Install monitoring devices at your electrical panel to track consumption by circuit
- **Solar Integration**: If you have solar panels, create dashboards and automations that optimize usage based on production
- **Load Shifting**: Develop automations that run high-consumption devices during off-peak hours or when renewable energy is abundant
- **Vampire Power Control**: Implement systems that automatically cut power to devices known to consume standby power when not in use
- **Consumption Goal Tracking**: Create visualization tools that gamify energy conservation with household goals and achievements

Multi-Factor Security Systems

Build layered security that combines multiple authentication methods:

- **Geofencing Plus Authentication**: Create security systems that consider both physical location and secondary authentication before disarming
- **Behavioral Analysis**: Develop systems that learn normal household patterns and alert for deviations
- **Progressive Security Levels**: Implement tiered security that adjusts based on occupancy, time of day, or vacation status
- **Simulated Occupancy 2.0**: Create sophisticated presence simulation that varies timing and activated devices to appear more natural
- **Neighborhood Security Network**: If neighbors also have smart homes, create opt-in shared alerts for suspicious activity

Custom Voice Control Projects

Extend voice capabilities beyond basic commands:

- **Custom Voice Assistant Personas**: Modify voice assistant responses with custom phrases and personalities
- **Multi-step Command Macros**: Create complex command sequences triggered by simple voice phrases
- **Voice-Activated Emergency Protocols**: Develop specific voice commands that trigger comprehensive emergency responses
- **Room-Specific Command Sets**: Configure different command libraries optimized for specific room functions

- **Voice Authentication**: Implement voice biometric verification for sensitive commands

Media and Entertainment Integration

Create immersive entertainment experiences:

- **Automatic Media-Based Scenes**: Design systems that adjust lighting, temperature, and even window coverings based on what's playing
- **Multi-Room Synchronized Audio**: Configure whole-home audio that can either play the same content everywhere or different content in different zones
- **Context-Aware Volume Control**: Develop smart volume adjustments that respond to ambient noise levels, time of day, or occupancy
- **Entertainment Voice Control**: Create custom voice commands specific to your media libraries and services
- **Activity-Based Media Suggestions**: Build systems that recommend content based on time of day, who's home, or other contextual factors

Custom Sensor Projects

Expand your home's awareness with DIY sensor implementations:

- **Water Usage Monitoring**: Install flow sensors on main water lines and major fixtures to track consumption and detect leaks

- **Custom Vibration Detection**: Create sensors that can monitor appliance operation through vibration patterns
- **Mail/Package Delivery Sensors**: Build detection systems for mailbox activity or package deliveries
- **Garden Soil Monitoring**: Implement moisture, light, and temperature sensors for garden beds with automated irrigation integration
- **Pet Activity Sensors**: Design monitoring systems for pet doors, food dishes, or water bowls that track pet routines

Accessibility Enhancements

Create customizations that make your smart home more accessible:

- **Visual Alert Systems**: Build light-based notification systems for those with hearing impairments
- **Alternative Interface Controls**: Implement switch, button, or touch controls for users who prefer non-voice interaction
- **Routine Assistance**: Develop reminder systems and guided activity sequences for users with cognitive challenges
- **Mobility Support**: Create automatic door operators, chair lifts, or other mobility assists controlled through smart home integration

- **Caregiver Remote Access**: Set up secure remote monitoring and control capabilities for family members or caregivers

Advanced Automation Logic

Implement more sophisticated decision-making in your automations:

- **Multi-condition Triggers**: Build automations that only activate when several conditions are simultaneously met
- **Adaptive Learning Systems**: Create automations that adjust their behavior based on patterns observed over time
- **Decision Tree Automation**: Implement if-then-else logic chains that can handle complex situational variations
- **Temporary Overrides**: Develop systems that allow for one-time exceptions to established routines without disrupting the underlying automation
- **Seasonal Adjustments**: Build automations that automatically adapt to seasonal changes in daylight, temperature, or household activities

Smart Kitchen Projects

Enhance your kitchen with advanced culinary technology:

- **Inventory Management**: Create systems using weight sensors or barcode scanners to track pantry and refrigerator contents
- **Recipe-Guided Cooking**: Build step-by-step cooking assistants that coordinate with smart appliances
- **Consumption Tracking**: Implement monitoring of regularly used items with automatic shopping list generation
- **Nutritional Analysis**: Develop systems that track meal ingredients and provide nutritional information
- **Smart Meal Planning**: Create meal suggestion systems based on available ingredients, dietary preferences, and previous meal history

Where to Go From Here

Your smart home journey is an ongoing evolution rather than a destination. As technologies advance and your needs change, you'll want to continue learning, adapting, and enhancing your systems. Here are valuable resources and strategies to support your continued growth in home automation expertise.

Online Communities and Forums

Connect with fellow enthusiasts to share ideas, solve problems, and stay current:

- **Reddit Communities**: Subreddits like r/homeautomation, r/smarthome, and platform-specific communities provide active discussion forums with users of all experience levels

- **Stack Exchange**: The Home Improvement and Internet of Things Stack Exchange communities offer structured Q&A formats for specific technical challenges
- **Discord Servers**: Many smart home platforms have dedicated Discord servers where users and sometimes developers interact in real-time
- **Facebook Groups**: Platform-specific and general smart home groups provide spaces for sharing projects and asking questions
- **Manufacturer Forums**: Official forums for products like Home Assistant, SmartThings, or Hubitat offer product-specific support and discussion

Advanced Learning Resources

Deepen your technical knowledge through structured learning:

- **Online Courses**: Platforms like Udemy, Coursera, and LinkedIn Learning offer courses on smart home technologies, programming for IoT, and related skills
- **YouTube Channels**: Creators focused on smart home topics provide tutorials, reviews, and project walkthroughs in accessible video formats
- **Technical Documentation**: Dive into the official documentation for your devices and platforms to

understand advanced features and integration options
- **Open Source Projects**: Explore GitHub repositories for home automation platforms to understand how they work and potentially contribute
- **Hackathons and Challenges**: Participate in IoT or smart home hackathons to solve specific problems within time constraints, accelerating your learning

Publications and Blogs

Stay informed about industry developments and innovations:

- **Dedicated Smart Home Publications**: Websites like Stacey on IoT, The Ambient, and Smart Home Geeks offer news and in-depth articles
- **Technology Review Sites**: CNET, Tom's Guide, and Wirecutter provide detailed reviews and comparative analyses of new products
- **Academic Research**: Google Scholar searches for "home automation" or "Internet of Things" can reveal cutting-edge research and future directions
- **Manufacturer Blogs**: Follow official blogs from companies like Google, Amazon, and Apple for announcements about platform changes
- **Industry Analysts**: Reports from firms like Gartner and Forrester can provide insight into market trends and emerging technologies

Professional Development Paths

Consider formalizing your knowledge for career opportunities:

- **Certification Programs**: Explore industry certifications from organizations like CEDIA (Custom Electronic Design & Installation Association)
- **Specialized Training**: Companies like Control4, Crestron, and Savant offer installer certification programs
- **Electrical Licensing**: Consider pursuing relevant electrical licensing if you're interested in installation work
- **Programming Skills**: Develop expertise in languages commonly used in home automation like Python, JavaScript, and C/C++
- **Networking Credentials**: CompTIA Network+ or Cisco certifications can strengthen your understanding of the network infrastructure critical to smart homes

Hands-On Expansion Opportunities

Apply your knowledge through practical projects and experiences:

- **Maker Spaces**: Join local maker communities where you can access tools, expertise, and collaborative opportunities

- **Home Shows and Expos**: Attend smart home exhibitions to see new products and speak directly with manufacturers
- **DIY Electronics Kits**: Explore Arduino, Raspberry Pi, or ESP32-based projects specifically designed for home automation
- **Beta Testing Programs**: Sign up for beta programs from smart home companies to preview and provide feedback on new features
- **Volunteer Opportunities**: Offer your expertise to community centers, assisted living facilities, or schools looking to implement smart technology

Sustainable and Ethical Considerations

Develop a thoughtful approach to technology adoption:

- **E-Waste Management**: Research proper disposal and recycling options for outdated smart home devices
- **Energy Efficiency Analysis**: Study the actual energy impact of your smart home systems to ensure they're delivering net benefits
- **Privacy Advocacy**: Follow organizations like the Electronic Frontier Foundation for information on digital privacy issues
- **Accessibility Resources**: Learn from organizations focused on technology accessibility to make your smart home inclusive

- **Right to Repair Movement**: Stay informed about consumer rights regarding the repair and modification of purchased devices

Future-Proofing Strategies

Prepare for the evolving technology landscape:

- **Open Standards Advocacy**: Follow and support the development of open standards like Matter and Thread that promote interoperability
- **Local Processing Focus**: Prioritize systems that can function without cloud dependencies to protect against service discontinuations
- **API Documentation**: Maintain documentation of the APIs your systems use to facilitate future migrations if needed
- **Configuration Backups**: Develop comprehensive backup strategies for all aspects of your smart home configuration
- **Upgrade Pathways**: Research modular systems that allow component upgrades without full system replacement

Community Contribution

Give back to the community that supports your growth:

- **Tutorial Creation**: Document your projects and share them through blogs, videos, or social media

- **Problem Solving**: Answer questions from beginners in online forums and communities
- **Open Source Contributions**: Contribute bug fixes, documentation, or features to open source home automation platforms
- **Local Workshops**: Organize or participate in community workshops that introduce others to smart home concepts
- **Code Sharing**: Publish your automation scripts, dashboards, or custom integrations for others to build upon

Integration with Emerging Technologies

Position yourself at the intersection of smart homes and other advancing technologies:

- **Artificial Intelligence**: Explore how machine learning can enhance pattern recognition and predictive capabilities in your home
- **Extended Reality**: Investigate applications of augmented and virtual reality for smart home visualization and control
- **Robotics**: Consider integration possibilities with household robots for cleaning, security, or assistance
- **Biomonitoring**: Research emerging technologies that connect health monitoring devices with home environmental controls
- **Renewable Energy**: Study integration of smart home systems with residential solar, battery storage, or electric vehicle charging

Personal Development Planning

Create a structured approach to your continued learning:

- **Skill Gap Analysis**: Identify specific technical or conceptual areas where you need additional knowledge
- **Project Roadmap**: Develop a prioritized list of future smart home projects based on value and complexity
- **Learning Schedule**: Allocate regular time for staying current with smart home developments
- **Documentation System**: Create your own knowledge base of solutions, configurations, and resources
- **Reflection Practice**: Periodically evaluate what's working well and what could be improved in your smart home

Your smart home journey represents the intersection of technology and personal lifestyle—a continuously evolving expression of how you want to live. By combining the technical foundation you've built with ongoing learning and community engagement, you're well-equipped to create a home that not only meets your current needs but can adapt to future technologies and life changes.

The most successful smart home implementers view their systems as perpetual works in progress, embracing both the challenges and opportunities that come with technological evolution. Each improvement not only enhances functionality but deepens your understanding and capabilities, creating a virtuous cycle of learning and implementation.

As you continue forward, remember that the ultimate measure of your smart home's success isn't its technical sophistication but how seamlessly it enhances your daily life, provides genuine convenience, and contributes to your wellbeing. Technology serves people, not the other way around—your smart home should always reflect your unique priorities, preferences, and values.

May your journey continue to be one of discovery, creativity, and satisfaction as your home becomes increasingly attuned to enhancing your quality of life.

Appendix Smart Sensing Devices and Their Functions

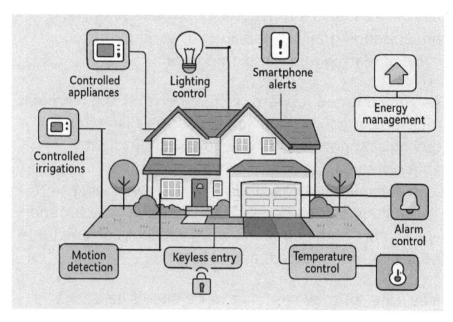

Smart Sensing Devices and Their Functions

1. Controlled Appliances

- Automates devices like washing machines, refrigerators, and ovens.

2. Lighting Control

- Manages lighting systems for energy saving and mood setting.

3. Smartphone Alerts

- o Sends real-time notifications (e.g., security alerts, device status).

4. **Energy Management**

   - o Monitors and optimizes energy usage across the house.

5. **Alarm Control**

   - o Triggers alerts during security breaches or emergencies.

6. **Temperature Control**

   - o Regulates heating and cooling systems based on preferences or weather.

7. **Keyless Entry**

   - o Allows door access via smartphone or biometric verification.

8. **Motion Detection**

   - o Detects movements for security and automation (like turning on lights).

9. **Controlled Irrigations**

   - o Manages garden watering systems based on soil moisture or schedules.

This figure provides a holistic view of how **IoT and smart sensors** can integrate into daily home operations for **enhanced convenience, efficiency, and security**.

Appendix Smart Wireless Security Systems

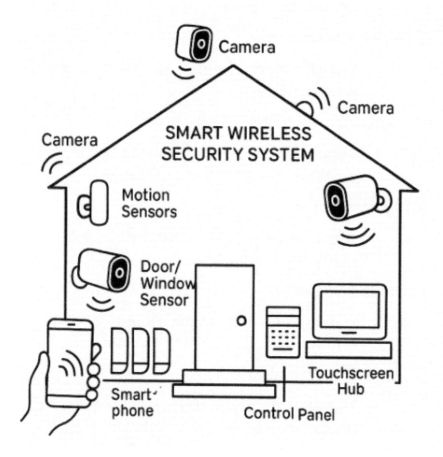

System Components Shown:

1. **Surveillance Cameras (top right):**

   - Outdoor bullet cameras

   - Used for 24/7 video monitoring

- connected to an NVR (Network Video Recorder)

2. **Motion Detectors (left and below cameras):**
   - Detects motion inside the home
   - Triggers alerts or sirens

3. **Window/Door Sensors (bottom left group):**
   - Monitors if a door or window is opened
   - Sends alerts when breached

4. **Control Panel/Keypad (center-right):**
   - Arms/disarms the system
   - Connects all devices

5. **Smartphone App Interface (handheld phone):**
   - Remote access to camera feed and controls
   - Real-time alerts and emergency button

6. **Touchscreen Monitor (bottom right):**
   - Central management system
   - connected to both cameras and sensors
   - Displays live feeds, controls system settings

7. **Network Video Recorder (under touchscreen):**
   - Stores recorded footage from all cameras
   - May include hard drive for long-term storage

Appendix Smart Bulb and Plug Wiring Diagram

Simple Smart Bulb Wiring Diagram

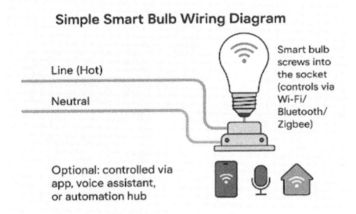

Line (Hot)

Neutral

Smart bulb screws into the socket (controls via Wi-Fi/ Bluetooth/ Zigbee)

Optional: controlled via app, voice assistant, or automation hub

Basic Smart Plug Wiring Diagram

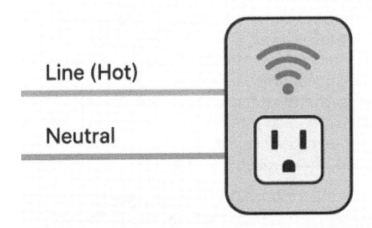

Line (Hot)

Neutral

Appendix Zigbee Layout

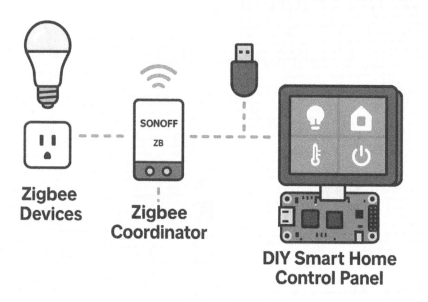

Zigbee Devices   **Zigbee Coordinator**   **DIY Smart Home Control Panel**

Zigbee is a wireless communication protocol designed specifically for low-power, low-data-rate applications like smart home devices and IoT (Internet of Things) systems. It enables various devices—such as lights, sensors, locks, thermostats, and alarms—to communicate with each other over a mesh network. In a mesh setup, each device can relay data, making the overall network more reliable and expandable.

Unlike Wi-Fi or Bluetooth, Zigbee uses very little power, allowing battery-powered devices to last for years. It operates on the IEEE 802.15.4 standard and typically functions on the 2.4 GHz frequency band, offering secure communication through AES-128 encryption.

Zigbee's biggest advantage lies in its scalability and robustness. As more Zigbee devices are added, the network grows stronger, not weaker. It's widely supported by smart home platforms like Amazon Echo, SmartThings, and Philips Hue. Overall, Zigbee offers an efficient and secure way to create a connected smart home ecosystem with minimal energy use

Appendix Z-Wave Layout

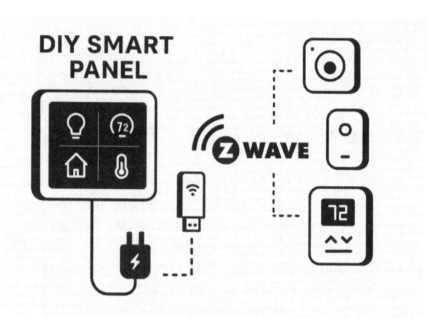

Z-Wave is a wireless communication protocol used in smart home and security devices to let them communicate with each other. It operates on a low-energy radio frequency (around 800-900 MHz), which helps it avoid interference with Wi-Fi and Bluetooth.

Z-Wave is commonly used in home automation systems to connect things like smart lights, door locks, motion sensors, thermostats, and security systems. One of its strengths is its mesh network—each Z-Wave device can relay signals to other devices, expanding the network range and improving reliability.

Compared to Wi-Fi, Z-Wave uses less power and is more stable for simple command-based tasks (like turning on lights or sending alerts). Devices using Z-Wave must be certified and compatible, which helps ensure smooth operation between different brands.

In security setups, Z-Wave is favored for its low latency, encryption, and reliability, making it a trusted choice for connecting sensors, hubs, and alarms.

Report: Mastering Home Automation: A DIY Guide to Smart Home Projects

As technology continues to transform modern living, *Mastering Home Automation: A DIY Guide to Smart Home Projects* arrives at the perfect time. This report examines emerging smart home trends, consumer preferences, and the importance of compatibility, security, and sustainability in home automation systems. With the rising demand for connected, efficient homes, this guide provides a practical approach for individuals seeking to create personalized smart home solutions without professional installation.

Market Trends & Consumer Preferences

Growing Demand for DIY Smart Home Solutions

Today's consumers are increasingly tech-savvy and eager to take control of their living spaces. With smart technology becoming more affordable and accessible, DIY smart home projects are on the rise. *Mastering Home Automation* empowers homeowners and hobbyists to build their own systems, providing clear, step-by-step instructions for projects involving lighting, security, climate control, and more.

This guide caters to individuals who value independence, creativity, and budget-friendly solutions, making it ideal for renters, homeowners, and tech enthusiasts alike.

Desire for Seamless Integration and Control

Consumers today prioritize systems that work together across platforms. Whether using voice assistants like Alexa or Google Home, or managing devices through centralized apps, seamless integration is key. *Mastering Home Automation* offers detailed tutorials and recommendations for choosing compatible hardware and software, ensuring readers can create a cohesive, centralized smart environment.

The guide also covers the importance of open-source platforms such as Home Assistant and Node-RED, giving users full control over customization and automation rules.

Security and Data Privacy Concerns

With the rise of connected devices, security and data privacy have become top concerns for consumers. *Mastering Home Automation* educates readers on the fundamentals of secure network setup, password management, device encryption, and local storage options. By focusing on best practices in cybersecurity, the guide builds confidence among readers who want to protect their homes and personal data.

Adherence to International Technology Standards

Creating a robust and reliable smart home requires adherence to globally recognized standards for communication, safety, and interoperability. *Mastering Home Automation* highlights the following standards to help readers design and implement systems that are future-proof and compliant with industry best practices.

IEEE 802.15.4 and Zigbee/Z-Wave Protocols

These wireless communication protocols are widely used for low-power smart home devices. *Mastering Home Automation* explains the role of Zigbee and Z-Wave in connecting devices such as sensors, locks, and thermostats, helping readers choose the right protocol based on range, speed, and device compatibility.

By following these protocols, users ensure their devices can communicate efficiently while minimizing interference and maximizing battery life.

Matter & Thread: The Future of Interoperability

Developed by major industry players (Apple, Google, Amazon), Matter is a new open-source standard designed to simplify smart home integration. *Mastering Home Automation* introduces readers to Matter and Thread, showcasing how these technologies promise a more unified and reliable smart home ecosystem.

By aligning projects with these emerging standards, readers can ensure long-term compatibility and avoid reliance on proprietary systems.

UL and CE Markings for Device Safety

When working with electrical components, safety is paramount. *Mastering Home Automation* provides guidance on identifying certified devices that meet UL (U.S.) and CE (European Union) safety standards. The book also emphasizes proper wiring practices, circuit protection, and load management to reduce the risk of fire, shock, or system failure.

Following these safety guidelines helps readers create smart home projects that are not only functional but also safe for everyday use.

Meeting Market Demand with Practical Knowledge

Today, the smart home market continues to expand at a rapid pace, driven by a desire for personalization, efficiency, and control. *Mastering Home Automation: A DIY Guide to Smart Home Projects* meets this demand by equipping readers with the technical knowledge and confidence to build their own solutions.

By incorporating:

- Practical project instructions
- Up-to-date technology trends
- International standards for safety and compatibility
- Cybersecurity best practices

...this guide becomes a vital resource for anyone looking to harness the power of smart technology in their own home.

As the smart home industry evolves, DIY enthusiasts are taking the lead in shaping their living environments. *Mastering Home Automation* bridges the gap between curiosity and capability, empowering readers to implement meaningful, customized solutions.

By aligning with recognized standards such as IEEE 802.15.4, Matter, and UL safety protocols, and by addressing the latest trends in integration, sustainability, and security, this guide ensures that DIYers are not just building smarter homes — they're building homes of the future.

"In a world driven by speed, convenience, and control, *Mastering Home Automation* isn't just a guide — it's your pathway to building a smarter, more empowered life, today and into the future."

Epilogue

The journey to mastering home automation is more than just installing smart devices—it's about creating a seamless, intuitive living space that enhances comfort, security, and efficiency. Throughout this guide, you've explored the fundamentals, tackled hands-on projects, and discovered how technology can transform your home into a dynamic, responsive environment.

But home automation doesn't end here. Technology evolves, new innovations emerge, and your needs will change over time. The beauty of a smart home lies in its adaptability. As you continue to refine and expand your setup, keep experimenting, learning, and pushing the boundaries of what's possible.

More than just convenience, home automation is about empowerment. It allows you to take control of your environment, customize your space, and embrace the future of living. Whether you're integrating advanced AI, optimizing energy efficiency, or simply finding new ways to make daily life smoother, your smart home will always be a work in progress—growing and evolving with you.

So, keep building, keep innovating, and most importantly, enjoy the smart home you've created.

Acknowledgments

I would like to express my deepest gratitude to everyone who has supported and inspired me throughout this journey of creating *Mastering Home Automation: A DIY Guide to Smart Home Projects*.

First and foremost, I thank my family for their unwavering patience and encouragement. Your belief in me, even when I was buried in wires and tech jargon, made this project possible.

To the countless DIY enthusiasts, innovators, and pioneers in the world of home automation—thank you for your tireless pursuit of progress and for sharing your knowledge. Your work has not only inspired me but has also laid the foundation for the ideas and projects discussed in this guide.

I also want to acknowledge the experts and industry professionals who have generously offered their insights and feedback. Your guidance has been invaluable, and your contributions have helped shape this book into something that I hope will inspire others to explore the world of home automation.

Lastly, to the readers—thank you for picking up this

book and investing your time and energy into creating your own smart home. You are the reason this book exists, and your dedication to making your living space more efficient and enjoyable is the true reward.

Author

Gerald S. Carolino is a passionate advocate for technology and innovation with over 29 years of experience in the engineering and HVAC industries. Holding degrees in Mechanical Engineering, Project Management, and Business Administration, Gerald has dedicated his career to integrating cutting-edge technology into practical, everyday applications. His commitment to continuous learning and problem-solving has led him to explore the world of home automation, where he has discovered the transformative power of smart home technologies.

In addition to his professional work, Gerald is a devoted family man and an active member of Toastmasters, where he shares his knowledge and enthusiasm for communication and leadership. As a writer and educator, he is dedicated to making complex ideas accessible and empowering others to embrace technology in their own lives.

When he's not working on home automation projects, Gerald enjoys spending time with his family, exploring new technologies, and sharing his knowledge through various platforms

.

Call to Action

Take Control of Your Smart Home Today!

Why wait to experience the convenience, security, and efficiency of a fully automated home? Whether you're a beginner or a tech enthusiast, this guide gives you step-by-step instructions to turn your house into a smarter, more connected space.

✓ **Save time & energy** with automation
✓ **Enhance security** with smart surveillance
✓ **Customize your home** with voice and app control

Start your first smart home project today! Grab your copy of *Mastering Home Automation* and bring your ideas to life. Your smarter home awaits!

"*A smart home doesn't start with devices — it starts with the desire to create, connect, and control your world, one project at a time.*"

www.ingramcontent.com/pod-product-compliance
Lightning Source LLC
LaVergne TN
LVHW022334060326
832902LV00022B/4040